The Place Remembered

Thomas Russel was the first settler in the Alton area. He arrived in 1834, attracted by potential farmland, dense woods, and abundant salmon in the cold, clear waters of the Credit River.

By 1857, Alton was well on its way to becoming an important industrial town. Two woollen mills, two grist mills, a saw mill, and factories producing axes and furniture were erected along the river banks, all deriving their basic power requirements from waterwheels set in Credit's tireless flow. But the river that made Alton also nearly destroyed it. In 1888, heavy rains washed out five dams, inundating the area and destroying mills and factories, many of which never recovered.

Alton Knitting Mills, however, not only managed to survive, it thrived. Under the ownership of the Dods family, the mill was expanded and improved in the early part of this century until it became one of the most modern knitting operations in Canada. Employing over 200 people at its peak, the mill produced soft, warm, 'O.K.' woollen underwear from New Zealand fleece that competed across the country with the well-known 'Stanfield's' products.

The advent of central heating, which reduced demands for 'woollies', together with the introduction of synthetic fibres and other technological advances finally stilled the Alton waterwheels and turbines in the 1960s.

Today, Alton is a peaceful village with more dreams than industries. Its current residents – and visitors – have rediscovered the charms that lured Thomas Russel in the first place: lush meadows, silent woods, and the still-sparkling waters of the river where it all began.

The Millcroft Inn

Fredy Stamm

COOKBOOK

The Porcupine's Quill, Inc.

Second printing, 1990.

Published by the Porcupine's Quill, Inc., 68 Main Street, Erin, Ontario N0B 1T0. Distributed by The University of Toronto Press, 5201 Dufferin Street, Downsview, Ontario M3H 5T8.

Interior photography is by Dennis Hall (The Niagara Studio, Toronto) who also provided the cover photograph. Occasional illustrations are by Virgil Burnett (Stratford).

Typeset in Galliard by The Coach House Press (Toronto). Printed by The Porcupine's Quill (Erin). Published in a first edition of 3000 copies in November 1987.

ISBN 0-88984-108-X

Contents

Fredy Stamm – Chef de Cuisine

A good chef must understand classical cuisine, which is the basis of all good cooking. I think it is essential for any professional cook to work in Europe to learn respect for the traditional methods.

• I don't believe in cooking trends. I do believe in the importance of adapting recipes to suit my guests' tastes. I like to develop a rapport with my clientele so they will allow me scope to tempt their palates with dishes not offered on the menu.

• I feel that the visual effect of food on a plate is almost as important as the taste. Dining should be a sensual experience. It is in the presentation that one can exercise creativity and imagination, and ultimately establish individuality.

• The profession demands devotion and stamina, which is no less than I expect of my staff. My usual working day is 12 to 14 hours, but I am well rewarded by an enthusiastic guest. For the cook at home, the preparation of a memorable meal will be time-consuming, and should not be abbreviated for convenience.

• Every food enthusiast should own a number of cookbooks written by top chefs, because cooking is a broad subject and forever changing. The comparison of chefs and their food is similar to rating restaurants and their ambiance. Cookbooks give you ideas which you can adapt to your own cooking style. Good cookbooks, with colour photographs, will also suggest presentations, which are so important to a successful meal. The most pedestrian lunch can suddenly blossom into haute cuisine with the correct implementation of colour.

• When selecting recipes for dinner parties, stick with tried and trusted dishes. If you want to experiment, prepare it for yourself first, and taste often while cooking.

• Do not be afraid to vary recipes to suit your own taste. Cooking is not done in books, but in your own kitchen.

• Before starting to cook, be sure that you have sufficient, and appropriate, ingredients and utensils.

• Prepare everything possible well in advance (your dinner guest will be amazed and delighted, if it takes a mere half an hour to 'whip up' a four-course meal).

• It is helpful to schedule a timetable, to write things down and cross them out when completed. This will ensure that meat, sauce and vegetables are all ready to go on the hot plate at the same time. Mental and physical organization are equally important.

• A successful meal starts with an organized shopping list, with substitutes identified should some items not be available at the market. Order 'exotic' ingredients well in advance. It will save you a lot of mental anguish and unnecessary footwork.

• Do not attempt difficult cutting and trimming of meats and fish on your own. Have your butcher or fishmonger perform these tasks to your specifications. They are professionally trained, and will be pleased to help.

• You will often find that the same recipe seldom turns out identically every time, although you should develop consistency once you have prepared a particular meal repeatedly, and have acquired a 'feel' for it.

• If at all possible, buy only fresh and seasonal ingredients. Tomatoes in January just aren't the same as tomatoes in August, but Canadian hot-house tomatoes in May may well be preferable to the American product, ripened in the back of a Kenworth trailer.

• In my kitchen I use only the freshest of ingredients, according to availability. In summer I grow most vegetables and herbs, and I am plentifully supplied with fresh meats, mushrooms and berries by local farmers.

Basics

Broths	Chicken Stock Crayfish Broth Veal or Lamb Jus (Brown Stock) Vegetable Broth
Mousselines	Chicken Salmon Veal
Sauces	Fresh Tomato Hollandaise Malossol
Vinaigrette	Red Pepper

Chicken Stock

5 lbs boiling chicken
20 cups cold water
1/8 cup diced carrots
2 tbsp diced onion
white of one leek
15 white peppercorns
2 sprigs chervil
1 bay leaf
1 clove
salt

Put the chicken in a large pot.
• Cover with the water. Bring slowly to the boil, skimming the surface constantly to remove the foam.
• Simmer for one hour.
• Add the carrot, onion and leek.
• Simmer for another two hours.
• Mix in the remaining ingredients for the final fifteen minutes. Season to taste.
• Remove the chicken*, and cool the stock in the refrigerator.
• Skim off the congealed fat and strain the stock thoroughly.
• To store, the stock may be frozen in individual air-tight containers, or in ice-cube trays and packed in plastic bags.

**Note:* Discard skin. Dice and refrigerate the chicken meat for use in soups, salads or sandwiches.

'Cooking and making love are the same, they both stem from the desire to give pleasure.'
Madame Lea

Crayfish Broth

*40 crayfish shells**
3 tbsp chopped shallots
3 tbsp chopped carrot
3 tbsp chopped celery
4 tomatoes, peeled
4 sprigs chopped dill
1 garlic clove, peeled
20 cups cold water
⅓ cup butter
1 clove

Oil a medium-sized pot and roast the shells over high heat for three minutes.
• Add the butter, and roast for another seven minutes over equally high heat.
• Add the remaining ingredients and cover with cold water. Let the broth simmer for thirty minutes.
• Force as much of the broth as possible through a fine sieve into a second pan. Use the back of a spoon to press the softened shells and vegetables through the sieve.
• Reduce the broth by half over medium heat, skimming the surface occasionally to remove foam. Refrigerate.
• Makes 10 cups.

Note: To store, freeze in ice cube trays and pack in plastic bags.

*Substitution: Try this recipe with lobster, substituting the chopped shells of two or three lobsters for the crayfish.

Veal or Lamb Jus (Brown Stock)

2 ½ cups white wine
20 cups water
2 lbs veal knuckle, or lamb bones
¼ cup diced carrot
¼ cup diced onion
¼ cup diced celery
2 chopped shallots
2 garlic cloves, peeled
½ cup tomato paste
2 sprigs fresh thyme
2 bay leaves
1 clove

Preheat oven to 350°F.

• Chop veal (or lamb) bones into walnut-sized pieces.

• Oil the bones very lightly and roast in the oven for 45 minutes. Stir frequently.

• Add the carrot, onion, celery, shallots and garlic. Roast for another thirty minutes, stirring frequently.

• Mix in the tomato paste and continue to roast for a further twenty minutes.

• Add the white wine in three stages, reducing the stock after each addition.

• Add the cold water with the remaining ingredients, simmering for a minimum of two hours. The stock will reduce to one-half the original quantity.

• Strain the stock through a double cheesecloth. Chill thoroughly, skim off the surface fat and refrigerate.

• Makes 10 cups.

Note: This recipe may be further reduced to achieve a stronger stock. Veal jus keeps well in the refrigerator for up to one week, or may be frozen in ice cube trays and stored in the freezer in plastic bags.

Use lamb jus exclusively for lamb dishes.

Vegetable Broth

20 cups water
1/4 cup carrot
1/8 cup onion
1/8 cup white leek
1/8 cup celery heart
12 white peppercorns
1/8 cup celery root
2 bay leaves
2 cloves

Clean and cube the vegetables.
• Put the vegetables with the seasonings in a stockpot, and cover with the water. Bring the broth rapidly to a boil.
• Lower the heat and reduce the broth to half the original quantity.
• Strain through a doubled cheesecloth; refrigerate.
• Makes 10 cups.

Note: This broth will keep in the refrigerator, covered, for several days. It may also be frozen in ice cube trays and stored in the freezer in plastic bags.

Chicken Mousseline

½ lb chicken breast
1 cup 35% cream
1 egg
1 egg yolk
⅛ cup white bread
a little milk

Skin and debone the chicken breast.
• Remove the crust from the bread. Cut into small cubes. Soak the bread in one to two tbsp of milk.
• Cut the chicken breast into small pieces. Mix with the egg and one tbsp of cream. Purée this mixture in a blender or food processor until smooth.
• Force the chicken purée and the soaked bread through a very fine sieve into a stainless steel bowl.
• Mount the bowl on crushed ice. Fold in the remaining cream, one tbsp at a time, and season to taste.
• Makes 2 cups.

'Couples who cook together stay together. (Maybe because they can't decide who'll get the Cuisinart.)'
Erica Jong

Salmon Mousseline

¼ lb pike
⅛ lb salmon
2 cups 35% cream
salt, pepper
2 eggs

Clean the fish.

• Reserve half of the cream. Purée remaining cream with all the other ingredients in a blender or food processor.

• Force the mousse through a very fine sieve into a stainless steel bowl.

• Mount the bowl on crushed ice.

• Fold the remaining cream into the mousse very slowly, one tbsp at a time.

• Season to taste, and chill.

• Makes 4 cups.

Veal Mousseline

¾ lb lean veal	Cut the veal into very small cubes.
⅔ cup 35% cream	• Crush the ice.
½ cup ice cubes	• Purée all ingredients in a blender or food processor.
2 eggs, salt, pepper	• Season to taste.
	• Makes 2 cups.

Fresh Tomato Sauce

1 lb fresh tomatoes
3 tbsp chopped shallots
1 tbsp chopped garlic
2 tsp fresh thyme, chopped
2 tsp marjoram, chopped
2 tsp oregano, chopped
1 ⅓ cups olive oil
1 ⅔ cups 35% cream
4 tsp fresh parsley, chopped

Preheat oven to 350°F.

• Core the tomatoes, and with a sharp knife score their bottoms. Drop in boiling water; cover the pan and simmer for thirty to 45 seconds. Remove and drain. Peel the tomatoes.

• Lightly oil a large iron casserole. Sauté the shallots, garlic and herbs over a moderate heat.

• Add tomatoes, cream, salt and pepper, blending well. Transfer the casserole to the oven and bake uncovered for two to three hours. Stir occasionally, adding more cream.

• Just before serving sprinkle with chopped parsley.

• Serves 6 to 8.

Note: Serve with your favourite pasta.

Hollandaise Sauce

2 oz chopped shallots
2 oz white vinegar
10 white peppercorns, crushed
2 oz white wine
6 egg yolks
2 1/2 cups butter
lemon juice
cayenne
salt

Melt the butter in a small pan over medium heat.
• Clarify by skimming the surface repeatedly and removing the milky residue from the bottom. Cool to lukewarm.
• Cover the shallots and the peppercorns with vinegar and bring rapidly to the boil. Reduce the liquid to a minimum.
• Combine the shallot-peppercorn residue with cold white wine and egg yolks in the top of a double boiler. Whisk until the sauce is creamy.
• Remove the top of the double boiler from the heat. Slowly whisk the lukewarm clarified butter into the sauce.
• Season with salt, cayenne and lemon juice. Strain the sauce through a cheesecloth.
• Keep in a warm place until serving.
• Serves 8 to 10.

Variation: For a sauce mousseline, fold whipped cream into the hollandaise.

Malossol Sauce

2 tsp chopped shallots
1 small bay leaf
1 clove
6 white peppercorns
2 cups champagne
1⅔ cups 35% cream
⅓ cup softened butter
chopped chervil
1 oz Beluga caviar
cayenne

Gently sweat the shallots, bay leaf, clove and peppercorns in a little butter for two minutes.
• Deglaze the pan with the champagne and reduce the sauce by two-thirds.
• Add the cream. Boil the sauce until it coats the back of a wooden spoon.
• Strain the sauce into a second pan and bring it back to the boil. Remove from heat.
• Whisk the butter into the hot sauce. Add the caviar and the chervil. Season with cayenne.
• Makes 2 cups.

Red Pepper Vinaigrette

1/8 cup onion	Peel the onion and trim the red pepper of seeds and membrane.
2 dill pickles	• Cut the onion, red pepper and dill pickle into small cubes.
4 tbsp capers	• Combine all ingredients except the oil and vinegar in a blender or food processor. Purée until smooth.
2 tsp chopped parsley	• Add the vinegar. Whisk the oil into the vinaigrette.
1 red pepper	• Season to taste with salt and pepper.
1 1/4 cups peanut oil	• Makes 2 cups (serves 8 to 10).
1/3 cup white vinegar	
salt, pepper	

'The greatest dishes are simple dishes.'
Auguste Escoffier

Appetizers

Country Salad with Hot Vinaigrette
Creamy Chicken Liver Terrine
with Rosemary
Frogs' Legs and Corn Ragoût
Marinated Salmon in Dill
Pheasant and Sweetbread Terrine
Roast Goat Cheese
with Sesame Seeds and Vinaigrette
Salmon-Stuffed Zucchini
with Lemon and Thyme Sauce
Sweet Onion and Garlic Tart
Warm Rabbit Salad with Rosemary

Country Salad with Hot Vinaigrette

1 head of Boston lettuce
*18 small bunches of lamb's lettuce**
6 Golden Delicious apples
10 strips bacon
36 walnut halves
red pepper vinaigrette *(see page 21)*

Trim and wash the greens carefully, discarding the outer leaves of the Boston lettuce. Spin dry.
• Peel and core the apples. Poach slowly in sugared lemon water until they are still a touch firm inside.
• Allow the apples to cool in the poaching water. Halve the apples; cut each half into six wedges.
• To make bacon-bits, cut the bacon into juliennes. Fry over medium heat until crisp.
• Arrange the salad on six chilled plates. Mound the greens in the centre of each plate. Flank each serving with twelve apple wedges, six on either side of the greens. Garnish with six walnut halves, three to each side.
• Warm the red pepper vinaigrette and drizzle over the salad.
• Sprinkle bacon-bits over the salad and serve promptly.
• Serves 6.

*Substitution: Try bibb or Boston if lamb's lettuce is not available.

'There is no love sincerer than the love of food.'
George Bernard Shaw

Creamy Chicken Liver Terrine with Rosemary

1 1/4 lbs chicken livers
3 eggs
3 egg yolks
4 tsp salt
1 chopped garlic clove
4 cups 35% cream
4 sprigs rosemary, chopped
black pepper, freshly ground

Preheat oven to 250°F.

• Trim the membrane from the chicken livers. Blend with the eggs, salt, garlic and rosemary in a food processor or blender.

• Strain through a fine sieve into a small bowl. Stir in the cream and whisk thoroughly.

• Season to taste with freshly ground black pepper.

• Pour into a shallow terrine.

• Cover the terrine securely: it must be airtight. Place in a very shallow waterbath (about 3/4″ of water) and poach for forty to fifty minutes.

• Serve with fresh melba toast and preserves.

• Serves 8 to 10.

Frogs' Legs and Corn Ragoût

20-24 frogs' legs
3 tbsp butter
1 cob sweet corn
3 tsp red pepper juliennes
3 tsp green peas
3 tsp chopped shallots
⅓ cup vegetable broth (see page 14)
⅔ cup 35% cream
salt, pepper
flour

Whip half the cream until stiff. Refrigerate.
• Trim fat and gristle from the frogs' legs and wash them well in cold water.
• Cut or grate the corn from the cob and cook the kernels in lightly salted water.
• In separate pots, cook the peas and red pepper juliennes for one minute in lightly salted water. Drain, cool and reserve.
• Season the frogs' legs and dust lightly with flour.
• Butter a skillet, fry the legs over medium heat for four minutes. Remove and keep warm.
• Quickly sweat the shallots in the same skillet. Add the vegetable broth and the remaining cream; bring to the boil. Reduce the sauce by two-thirds.
• Toss in the vegetables. Season to taste. Keep warm.
• Arrange the frogs' legs attractively on four heated plates.
• Remove sauce from heat and fold in the whipped cream. Ladle the sauce in equal portions over the ragoût, and serve immediately.
• Serves 4. See photograph opposite page 30.

'Three million frogs' legs are served in Paris daily. Nobody knows what became of the rest of the frogs.'
Fred Allen

Marinated Salmon in Dill

3/8 cup rock salt
1/8 cup sugar
20 white peppercorns, crushed
4 sprigs dill, chopped
1 lemon, juiced
1 tsp mustard seed
4 lbs fresh salmon

Mix the ingredients of the marinade together, but save the lemon juice for later.

• Clean and debone the salmon without detaching the skin. Halve the salmon lengthwise.

• Rub each piece thoroughly with the marinade, and drizzle with lemon juice.

• Place one salmon half on a large platter, skin side down. Position the second half on top, skin side up.

• Cover with a wooden board and weight with a heavy object.

• Refrigerate for at least 48 hours. Turn the fish every eight hours to marinate each side equally.

• For a garnish, mix whipped cream with horseradish, salt and pepper. Serve the salmon in thin slices, accompanied by this sauce.

• Serves 6.

Pheasant and Sweetbread Terrine

2 lbs lean pheasant
1 ¾ lbs sweetbreads
⅛ cup whole hazelnuts
1 ⅔ cups 35% cream
2 tsp salt
10 oz spinach
3 tbsp cognac
black pepper, freshly ground
5 oz sliced backfat

Preheat oven to 350°F.

• Immerse the sweetbreads in cold running water. Remove the skin, fat and blood vessels. Cut into small pieces.

• Roast the peeled hazelnuts lightly in a little butter. Chop coarsely.

• Clean the spinach thoroughly, discarding stalks and discoloured leaves. Cook in lightly salted water for two minutes and chop very finely.

• Force the pheasant meat through a meat grinder at the finest possible grade.

• Combine all ingredients but the backfat. Refrigerate for one hour.

• Line a terrine with slices of backfat. Fill the terrine with the meat mixture, and cover with remaining backfat slices.

• Place in a shallow waterbath (one-half to one inch of water) and cook in the oven for one hour.

• Serves 8.

Roast Goat Cheese with Sesame Seeds and Vinaigrette

*6 x 3½ oz goat cheeses**
1 tsp sesame seeds
⅓ cup red pepper vinaigrette (see page 21)
lamb's lettuce†

Preheat oven to 400°F.
• Place the cheeses on a baking tray and roast in a hot oven for five minutes.
• Toast the sesame seeds under the broiler.
• Heat the vinaigrette.
• Carefully transfer each of the softened cheeses to a heated dinner plate. Sprinkle liberally with sesame seeds.
• Garnish with lamb's lettuce and drizzle with the hot vinaigrette. Serve with melba toast.
• Serves 6.

*Substitutions: 100% goat cheese is strongly flavoured. Half-and-half cheese, which is much milder, may be preferable.

†Lamb's lettuce can be found at specialty greengrocers. If not available, try bibb or Boston lettuce.

Salmon-Stuffed Zucchini with Lemon and Thyme Sauce

8 small zucchini, blossoms intact
1/2 cup salmon mousseline *(see page 16)*
2/3 cup vegetable broth *(see page 14)*
1/3 cup 35% cream
1/4 cup softened butter
chopped thyme
salt, pepper
1 lemon

Wash and trim the zucchini, carefully rinsing the inside of each blossom. Do not detach the blossoms.
• Fill a piping bag with salmon mousseline and gently stuff each blossom. Press the petals forward onto the mousseline to create a quenelle.
• Bring the vegetable broth to the boil. Place the zucchini carefully in the pan.
• Steam the zucchini, covered, for five minutes over medium heat. Remove from the pan and keep warm.
• Quickly reduce the vegetable broth to a minimum. Stir in the cream and the lemon juice.
• Add the chopped thyme and cook for one more minute. Turn off the heat.
• Whisk the softened butter into the hot sause.
Season to taste.
• Place two zucchini on each heated plate.
Cover with sauce.
• Serves 4. See photograph opposite this page.

Sweet Onion and Garlic Tart

4 cups all-purpose flour
14 *tbsp butter*
1 *egg yolk*
⅔ *cup water*
2 *tsp salt*
1 *tsp white vinegar*

The pastry: Preheat oven to 400°F.

• Rub flour and butter together thoroughly. Add the egg yolk, water, vinegar and salt and work the dough into a ball. Refrigerate in plastic wrap for one hour.

• On a lightly floured surface, roll out the dough to fit a nine inch flan. (Choose a pan with a removable fluted rim.) When the pastry is an eighth of an inch thick, drape it carefully over the rolling pin and lower into the flan. Press firmly. Prick the bottom with a fork.

• Bake at 400°F. for approximately thirty minutes. (To prevent excessive shrinking line the pastry with waxed or parchment paper, one inch larger than the flan and fill the cavity with dried lentils. After pre-baking, remove paper and lentils.) While the pastry is baking, prepare the filling.

1⅔ *cups 35% cream*
¾ *cup milk*
2 *eggs*
4 *egg yolks*
2 *tbsp butter*
1 *cup sweet red onions*
5 *garlic cloves, chopped*
a handful of chives, chopped
salt, pepper
nutmeg

The filling: Peel and chop the onion.

• Lightly butter a skillet. Sweat the onion and garlic gently over medium heat until tender.

• Mix together the cream, milk and eggs. Season to taste with salt, pepper and nutmeg.

• Pour the batter into the flan. Bake at 320°F. for one hour. If necessary, cover the tart with tin foil for the final twenty minutes to prevent scorching.

• Serves 8.

Warm Rabbit Salad with Rosemary

6 rabbit loins
2 tsp olive oil
2 tbsp unsalted butter
salt, pepper
paprika

The rabbit: Clean and trim the rabbit loins.
• Heat oil and butter together in a skillet.
• Slowly roast the seasoned loins over moderate heat until medium rare. Remove the loins and keep them warm. Do not discard the pan juices.

1 tsp chopped shallots
4 sprigs rosemary, chopped
⅓ cup vegetable broth *(see page 14)*
⅓ cup olive oil
⅛ cup sherry vinegar
salt, pepper

The dressing: Add the shallots and the rosemary to the same skillet. Sweat them gently in the rabbit juices for half a minute.
• Deglaze the pan with the vegetable broth, reducing the sauce to a minimum.
• Remove the pan from the heat and allow it to cool.
• Whisk in the vinegar, then the oil. Season to taste.

⅛ cup celery root juliennes
½ red onion
juice of 1 lemon
olive oil
salt, pepper
1 head of Boston lettuce

The salad: Slice the onion finely and mix with the celery root juliennes.
• Toss the vegetables with the lemon juice, a little olive oil, salt and pepper.
• Marinate for ten minutes.
• Divide the Boston lettuce into six portions. Top each portion with celery-onion marinade.
• Cut each of the warmed rabbit loins into four long strips and arrange attractively over the lettuce.
• Drizzle with the warm dressing and serve promptly.
• Serves 6.

Soups

Asparagus and Broccoli Soup
Clear Chicken Soup
with Vegetables and Chanterelles
Cream of Artichoke Soup
with Smoked Salmon
Cream of Pumpkin Soup
Gazpacho
Gooseberry Soup
Roasted Flour Soup with *Sbrinz*
Vegetable Velouté

Asparagus and Broccoli Soup

20 asparagus tips
10 broccoli flowerets

The garnish: Cook broccoli flowerets and asparagus tips for one minute in lightly salted water then chill in ice water immediately. Slice the asparagus tips in half, lengthwise. Reserve.

20 green asparagus stalks
3/4 cup broccoli flowerets
1/8 cup diced potato
8 cups chicken stock *(see page 11)*
4 sprigs fresh thyme
1/3 cup softened butter
salt, pepper
1 lemon

The soup: Clean and prepare the vegetables for the soup. Dice the asparagus stalks.
• Gently sweat the vegetables with the thyme in one tbsp of butter for five minutes.
• Add the chicken stock and bring to the boil. Cook for twenty-five minutes, uncovered.
• Force the soup through a fine sieve, pressing the cooked vegetables with the back of a spoon. If necessary, add some vegetable broth (see page 14).
• Bring to the boil. Remove from heat and whisk in the softened butter. Season to taste.
• Serve in heated bowls. Garnish with re-heated asparagus tips and broccoli flowerets, a few thyme leaves and a little grated lemon rind.
• Serves 10.

Note: This soup is delicious chilled. Proceed as above, omitting the softened butter. Allow the soup to cool; blend with yoghurt to taste. Refrigerate. Serve in chilled bowls and decorate with a chilled garnish.

'In any world menu, Canada must be considered the vichyssoise of nations – it's cold, half-French, and difficult to stir.' *Stuart Keate*

Clear Chicken Soup with Vegetables and Chanterelles

1 five lb boiling chicken
20 cups cold water
$1/8$ cup diced carrot
2 tbsp diced onion
the white of one leek
15 white peppercorns
2 sprigs chervil
1 bay leaf
1 clove
salt

The chicken: Put the chicken in a large pot.
• Cover with water. Bring slowly to the boil, skimming the surface constantly to remove foam.
• Simmer for one hour.
• Add the carrot, onion, leek, and the chanterelle stalks. Simmer for another two hours.
• Mix in the remaining ingredients for the final fifteen minutes.
• Remove the chicken, and when cool remove the skin.
• Cut the breast meat into thin slices; julienne the leg meat.
• Strain the soup very carefully through a doubled cheesecloth. Keep the soup hot.

$1/3$ cup chanterelles, sliced (caps only)
$1/8$ cup carrot juliennes
$1/8$ cup celery juliennes
$1/8$ cup turnip juliennes
$1/8$ cup fresh peas

The garnish: Gently sauté the chanterelle caps in a little butter for two minutes.
• Cook the vegetables (each separately) in slightly salted water, retaining crispness, about one minute.

Presentation: Divide the meat and vegetable garnish in equal portions, and place into heated soup bowls.
• Cover with hot soup.
• For a final touch, float a few chervil leaves on top.
• Serve immediately.
• Serves 10.

Cream of Artichoke Soup with Smoked Salmon

10 artichoke hearts
1/4 cup diced potato
2/3 cup champagne
8 cups chicken stock (see page 11)
2 cups 35% cream
1/3 cup softened butter
1/4 cup smoked salmon juliennes

Clean the artichokes and dice the potato. Sweat the vegetables gently in a little butter for five minutes.
• Add the champagne and the chicken stock, and simmer for twenty minutes.
• Cool briefly; purée the soup in a blender or food processor. Force through a fine sieve, pressing the vegetables with the back of a spoon.
• Stir in the cream and bring the soup back to the boil. Simmer for fifteen minutes.
• Remove from heat. Whisk the softened butter into the hot soup.
• Serve immediately in heated bowls. Garnish with juliennes of smoked salmon.
• Serves 6.

Note: This soup chills beautifully. Follow the instructions above, omitting the softened butter. Allow the soup to cool before refrigerating overnight or for twenty-four hours. Serve in chilled bowls, garnished with smoked salmon juliennes.

Cream of Pumpkin Soup

10 oz pumpkin-meat
1/8 cup celery root
1/3 cup kohlrabi, or other turnip
1/2 cup white leek
1/2 cup potato
8 tomatoes, peeled and seeded
16 cups chicken stock *(see page 11)*
2 cups 35% cream
1/3 cup softened butter
salt, pepper, cayenne
pumpkin seeds, roasted
chervil leaves
cinnamon

Clean and dice the vegetables.
• Sweat the vegetables in one tbsp butter for fifteen minutes over medium heat. Add the pumpkin-meat.
• Add the chicken stock; cover. Simmer for one hour.
• Cool the soup briefly, then purée in a blender or food processor. Force the purée through a fine sieve into a second pot.
• Stir in the cream and bring the soup to the boil. Remove from heat. Whisk the softened butter into the hot soup.
• Season with the spices.
• Serve the soup in heated bowls. Decorate each portion with chervil leaves and roasted pumpkin seeds.
• Serves 10.

Note: The flavour of this soup is enhanced when it is prepared twenty-four hours in advance. Proceed as directed until the cream has been blended into the soup; then refrigerate for twenty-four hours or overnight. Complete the final steps directly before serving.

Gazpacho

2 English cucumbers
2 red peppers
1 Spanish onion
1 ½ cups peeled, seeded tomatoes
4 large garlic cloves
6 tbsp tomato paste
4 cups tomato juice
1⅔ cups olive oil
⅔ cup red wine vinegar
salt, pepper

Clean the vegetables and chop them coarsely.
• Purée the vegetables with the tomato paste in a blender or food processor.
• Stir in the tomato juice and the vinegar.
• Slowly whisk in the olive oil. Chill the soup for a minimum of four hours to develop flavour.
• Top with roasted croutons.
• Serve with a selection of garnishes in separate bowls: chopped tomatoes, chopped cucumbers, and diced red peppers.
• Serves 6.

Gooseberry Soup

6 cups fresh gooseberries
4 cups water
4 cups champagne
⅔ cup sugar
3 tbsp cornstarch
cinnamon
salt

Wash the gooseberries carefully.
• Cover the berries with the water and the champagne. Bring to the boil and simmer until all of the berries have burst.
• Force through a fine sieve, pressing the berries with the back of a metal spoon.
• Add the sugar, salt and cinnamon. Bring the soup back to the boil.
• Dissolve the cornstarch in a little cold water. Stir into the boiling soup. Cook for one more minute, until the soup becomes thick and glossy.
• Serve hot or cold. Roasted bread croutons make an excellent garnish.
• Serves 15.

Roasted Flour Soup with Sbrinz

2 1/2 cups all-purpose flour
1/3 cup unsalted butter
2 large onions, sliced
8 pints chicken stock (see page 11)
3 tbsp Sbrinz, or grated parmesan
salt, pepper

Roast the flour in a dry pan until lightly browned.
• Melt the butter in a skillet. Sweat the onions for fifteen minutes over medium heat.
• Stir in the roasted flour, then the chicken stock.
• Simmer for ninety minutes, seasoning to taste.
• Garnish with a sprinkle of grated cheese.
• Serves 10.

Note: This very traditional and extremely hearty Swiss soup may be kept in the refrigerator – without the cheese – for up to seven days.

Vegetable Velouté

2/3 cup white leek
2/3 cup carrot
2/3 cup rutabaga
1/3 cup celery root
1 large potato
4 tomatoes, peeled and seeded
10 cups chicken stock *(see page 11)*
1 1/2 cups 35% cream
1/3 cup softened butter
chervil leaves
salt, pepper

Clean and dice the vegetables.
• Sweat the leek, carrot, rutabaga and celery root in a little butter for five minutes.
• Add chicken stock, cover, and simmer for twenty minutes.
• Add the tomatoes and the potato. Bring the soup back to the boil and simmer for a further twenty minutes.
• Remove from heat and allow the soup to cool briefly. Purée in a blender or food processor. Refrigerate for twenty-four hours.*

• *The following day:* mix the cream into the soup and bring to the boil. Remove from heat, and whisk the softened butter into the hot soup.
• Serve immediately in heated bowls.
Garnish with chervil.
• Serves 8 to 10.

Variation: This soup provides the base for *Black Truffles in Vegetable Velouté.* Add one black truffle, brushed and thinly sliced, per serving, for the final ten minutes of cooking time.

*Vegetable soups should be refrigerated for 24 hours to develop full flavour.

Fish

Chartreuse of Salmon with Beluga Caviar
Fillet of Red Snapper
with Bone Marrow and Rosemary
Fillet of Turbot with Smoked Salmon
Medallion of Grouper with Anise
Medallion of Monkfish
with Crayfish *à la provençale*
Paupiette of Salmon and Pike
with Chanterelles and Red Wine Butter
Ragoût of Eel *à l'espagnole*
Salmon Soufflé with Parsley Cream Sauce
Steamed Pickerel Fillets on Pine Needles

*Chartreuse of Salmon with Beluga Caviar**

6 five oz round molds
1 cup salmon mousseline (see page 16)
1/8 cup carrot juliennes
1/8 cup rutabaga juliennes
1/8 cup red pepper juliennes
1/8 cup yellow pepper juliennes
1/8 cup snow pea juliennes
2 oz Beluga caviar
Malossol sauce (see page 20)

Preheat oven to 350°F.

• Blanch each of the julienned vegetables separately in lightly salted water.

• Butter the molds liberally. Line the bottom and sides of each mold with the juliennes, alternating colours.

• Fit a piping bag with a medium tip. Pipe the mousseline carefully into the molds to cover the bottom and the sides. Leave a hollow in the centre.

• Divide the caviar among the six hollows. Cover with the remaining mousseline.

• Set the molds in an ovenproof pan. Add an inch of water and place in the oven. Poach for eight minutes. Unmold immediately.

• Serve on a bed of Malossol Sauce.

• Serves 6. See photograph opposite page 54.

*Substitution: Salmon caviar is a good alternative.

'Fish, to taste right, must swim three times – in water, in butter and in wine!' *Polish Proverb*

Fillet of Red Snapper with Bone Marrow and Rosemary

4 five oz red snapper fillets
2 oz bone marrow
⅔ cup veal jus (see page 13)
⅔ cup red wine
⅓ cup 35% cream
3 tsp chopped shallots
⅓ cup softened butter
juice of half a lemon
3 sprigs fresh rosemary, chopped

Wash the marrow in cold water and slice thinly.
• Scale the snapper fillets, being careful to leave the skin intact.
• Fry the fillets over medium heat: skin side up for four minutes, and skin side down for two minutes.
• Remove fillets and keep them warm.
• Add a little butter to the pan and lightly sweat the shallots and the rosemary for one minute.
• Deglaze the pan with the red wine and the veal jus.
• Stir in the cream and the bone marrow. Allow the sauce to simmer for another two minutes.
• Remove the marrow. Distribute in equal portions over four warmed plates.
• Remove the sauce from the heat and whisk in the lemon juice, then the softened butter.
• Spoon the sauce generously over marrow and top each serving with a warm red snapper fillet. Serve immediately.
• Serves 4.

Fillet of Turbot with Smoked Salmon

*4 five oz turbot fillets**
*1/4 cup smoked salmon juliennes**
3 tsp chopped shallots
1 bay leaf
1 1/4 cups champagne
1 1/4 cups 35% cream
1/2 cup softened butter
chopped parsley
cayenne
salt

Sprinkle the shallots and the bay leaf over a lightly buttered pan. Add the champagne.

• Bring the broth to a gentle simmer. Remove and discard the bay leaf.

• Poach the turbot fillets lightly for four minutes in the broth. Remove the fillets, cover, and keep warm.

• Reduce the stock by two-thirds.

• Stir in the cream and reduce again by two-thirds; add the smoked salmon juliennes at midpoint.

• Place one turbot fillet on each of four warmed plates. Remove the juliennes from the sauce and distribute evenly over the fish.

• Remove the sauce from the heat and whisk in the softened butter. Add the chopped parsley, salt and cayenne to taste.

• Cover each fillet generously with sauce. Serve.

• Serves 4.

*Substitution: For best results, choose turbot of European origin and Scottish smoked salmon.

Medallion of Grouper with Anise

4 five oz grouper fillets
3 tsp chopped shallots
1 tsp anise seed
⅓ cup dry vermouth
⅓ cup white wine
⅓ cup 35% cream
⅓ cup softened butter
⅛ cup fennel juliennes
1 sprig dill, chopped
salt, pepper

Gently sweat the fennel juliennes and the dill in a little butter until tender. Remove from the pan and distribute over four warmed plates. Keep warm.
• Add a little butter to the same pan. Sauté the shallots and the anise seed for one minute.
• Add the grouper and sauté for two minutes. Deglaze the pan with vermouth and white wine.
• Allow the fish to simmer in the sauce, covered, for four to five minutes over medium heat.
• Remove the fish. Centre each portion on the fennel juliennes; keep warm.
• Add the cream to the sauce and reduce by two-thirds.
• Remove the sauce from the heat and whisk in the softened butter. Season to taste.
• Ladle the sauce over the grouper. Garnish with fennel fern.
• Serves 4.

Medallion of Monkfish with Crayfish à la provençale

12 two oz monkfish, cut in medallions
1 2/3 cups crayfish broth (see page 12)
1/4 cup carrot paysanne
1/4 cup white leek paysanne
1/4 cup celery root paysanne
1/4 cup green peas
12 crayfish

The medallions: Cook each of the vegetables separately in lightly salted water. Cool, drain, and reserve the vegetables.
• Cook the crayfish in lightly salted water. Cool. Remove the tail meat and reserve for use as a garnish.
• Gently poach the medallions of monkfish in crayfish broth for three to five minutes.
• Remove the monkfish. Reduce the broth by one-half and add the vegetables. Keep warm.

1/4 cup white bread crumbs
1 tsp chopped garlic
2 tsp chopped shallots
1 sprig chopped rosemary
1 sprig chopped thyme
4 sprigs chopped parsley
2/3 cup melted butter
salt, pepper

The provençale: Sauté the shallots, garlic and herbs in a little butter for two minutes. Add the remaining butter and the white breadcrumbs.
• Season to taste.

The presentation: Top each monkfish medallion with the provençale and brown lightly under the broiler.
• Distribute the broth and the vegetables over four warmed soup plates.
• Place three medallions on each plate, garnish with crayfish tail meat, and serve.
• Serves 4.

Paupiette of Salmon and Pike with Chanterelles and Red Wine Butter

½ lb salmon
½ lb pike
16 large chanterelle mushrooms
8 large savoy cabbage leaves
4 tsp unsalted butter
chopped parsley
salt, pepper

The paupiettes: Preheat oven to 350°F.
• Clean the fish and cut into three-quarter inch cubes.
• Cut twelve chanterelles into small cubes. Gently sauté the mushrooms for two minutes in a little butter.
• Blanch the cabbage leaves in lightly salted water until flexible, but not soft.
• Mix the chanterelles and the cubed fish together, seasoning with salt and pepper. Place half a cup of this mixture in the centre of each cabbage leaf and wrap the leaf tightly to form a longish paupiette. (The finished paupiette will resemble a thin, untidy football.) Allow two paupiettes per serving.
• Place the paupiettes in a little butter on a cast-iron pan. Roast in the oven for seven to nine minutes; keep warm.

2 chopped shallots
⅔ cup full-bodied red wine
⅓ cup Port
⅓ cup Madeira
⅔ cup softened butter
salt, pepper

The butter: Sauté the shallots in a little butter for one minute.
• Add the wines. Reduce the sauce by two-thirds.
• Remove the sauce from the heat and whisk in the softened butter.

The presentation: Ladle the hot sauce onto four warmed plates. Serve the paupiettes on the sauce. Sauté the remaining chanterelles in a little butter and use as a garnish.
• Serves 4.

Ragoût of Eel à l'espagnole

*1 1/4 lb eel**
4 tbsp chopped onion
3 tsp chopped shallots
1 tsp chopped garlic
2 chopped red peppers
5 chopped green olives
5 chopped black olives
6 peeled tomatoes, seeded and chopped
1/3 cup virgin olive oil
2/3 cup dry white wine
2 oz red wine
salt, pepper
paprika

Clean the eel and cut into one inch slices.

- Sauté the eel in very hot olive oil for two minutes.
- Add the vegetables. Continue to sauté over high heat for three more minutes.
- Add both wines, simmering for an additional two minutes.
- Season to taste. Serve over rice pilaf.
- Serves 4.

*Substitution: Shrimp makes an interesting alternative.

Salmon Soufflé with Parsley Cream Sauce

4 three oz salmon medallions
1 1/4 cups salmon mousseline *(see page 16)*
4 egg whites
2/3 cup white wine
3 tsp chopped shallots
1 1/4 cups 35% cream
1/3 cup softened butter
3 tbsp Italian parsley leaves
salmon caviar
salt, pepper

Preheat oven to 400°F.

• Purée the parsley in a blender or food processor with a little water. Reserve.

• Beat the egg whites until stiff. Fold slowly into the salmon mousseline.

• Cover the surface of each medallion with an equal amount of soufflé. Use a metal spatula to round and level the soufflé layers evenly.

• Lightly butter an ovenproof pan, sprinkle with shallots and add the white wine. Carefully position the soufflé medallions in the pan.

• Braise the soufflés in a hot oven for seven minutes, or until very lightly browned.

• Remove the soufflés and keep warm.

• Bring the braising liquid to the boil and stir in the cream.

• Reduce the sauce until it coats the back of a wooden spoon.

• Add the parsley juice and bring the sauce back to the boil. Turn off the heat. Whisk the softened butter into the hot sauce. Season to taste.

• Serve each soufflé on a warm plate in a pool of sauce. Garnish with salmon caviar.

• Serves 4.

Steamed Pickerel Fillets on Pine Needles

4 five oz pickerel fillets
1 branch pine needles
3 tsp chopped shallots
1/8 cup carrot juliennes
1/8 cup celery root juliennes
1/8 cup rutabaga juliennes
1/8 cup leek juliennes
1/8 cup red pepper juliennes
2/3 cup dry white wine
2/3 cup 35% cream
1 lemon, juiced
1/3 cup softened butter
salt, pepper

Crush the pine needles with a rolling pin.
• Butter a large pan generously and sprinkle with the chopped shallots.
• Lay the pine needles in the pan and cover with cheesecloth.
• Layer the vegetable juliennes to create a bed. Place the pickerel fillets on the vegetables.
• Pour the lemon juice and the wine over the fish.
• Cover, and bring rapidly to the boil. Steam the fish until tender: five to seven minutes.
• Remove the fillets and the vegetables. Distribute the vegetables attractively over four warmed plates, top with the fillets and keep warm.
• Strain the stock into a second pan. Reduce by one-half.
• Stir in the cream. Over high heat, reduce the sauce by two-thirds.
• Remove from heat. Whisk the softened butter into the hot sauce and season to taste. Ladle the sauce over the pickerel fillets, and serve.
• Serves 4. See photograph opposite this page.

Crustaceans

Bay Scallops with Vegetables and Vermouth
Crayfish Ragoût
with Broccoli and Cauliflower
Lobster and Scallop 'Stew' with Saffron
Rendez-vous of Oysters
and Calves' Brains 'Dom Perignon'
Salade Neptune
Shrimp with Soy Sauce and Ginger

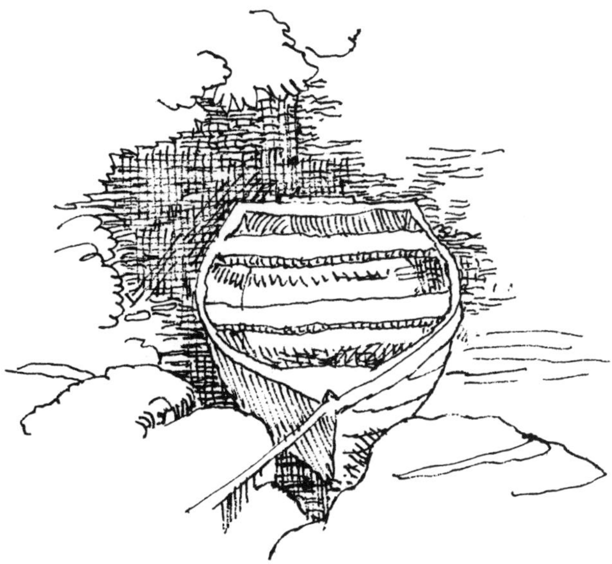

Bay Scallops with Vegetables and Vermouth

1 lb bay scallops
1/8 cup carrot juliennes
1/8 cup white leek juliennes
1/8 cup celery root juliennes
1/8 cup snow pea juliennes
3 tbsp chopped shallots
1/3 cup dry vermouth
1/3 cup 35% cream
1/3 cup softened butter
chopped chives
salt, pepper
olive oil

Prepare a cast-iron skillet with olive oil. Sear the scallops over very high heat for half a minute.
• Remove the scallops with a slotted spoon; keep warm.
• Add a little butter to the skillet and slowly cook the vegetable juliennes for two minutes. Remove and keep warm.
• Deglaze the pan with the vermouth and reduce the sauce to half the original quantity.
• Stir in the cream. Reduce the sauce quickly, until it coats the back of a wooden spoon. Add the chopped chives.
• Remove the sauce from the heat and whisk in the softened butter.
• Fold in the scallops and season to taste.
• Arrange the scallops on four warmed plates. Ladle the sauce over each serving and garnish with the warm vegetable juliennes.
• Serves 4.

'The stuff that dreams are made of usually comes out of the refrigerator around midnight.'
Jack Wasserman

Crayfish Ragoût with Broccoli and Cauliflower

40 crayfish
1 2/3 cups crayfish broth (see page 12)
1/3 cup champagne
1/3 cup softened butter
1/4 cup firm broccoli
1/4 cup cauliflower
1/8 cup butter
chopped parsley
salt, pepper
cayenne

Separate the broccoli and cauliflower into small flowerets.

• Clean the crayfish; cook in lightly salted water for one minute. Cool.

• Remove the tail meat; set aside.

• Melt one oz of butter in a cast-iron skillet. Cook the cauliflower and broccoli flowerets slowly for eight to ten minutes. Season with salt, pepper and chopped parsley.

• Reheat the crayfish in the broth. Prepare a bed of broccoli and cauliflower flowerets in four soup plates and distribute the crayfish over the vegetables. Keep warm.

• Add the champagne to the crayfish broth and reduce by three-quarters. Remove from heat.

• Whisk in the softened butter. Season with cayenne.

• Ladle the sauce over the crayfish and serve immediately.

• Serves 4. See photograph opposite this page.

Lobster and Scallop 'Stew' with Saffron

2 large lobsters
16 large scallops
1/4 cup savoy cabbage paysanne
3 tsp chopped shallots
1/3 cup dry vermouth
1/3 cup champagne
1 2/3 cups crayfish broth (see page 12)
1/3 cup softened butter
generous pinch of saffron

Cook the lobsters in lightly salted water until tender (ten to fifteen minutes).
• Cool. Remove claw and tail meat, cutting the tail meat into half-inch slices. Reserve the broth.
• Blanch the cabbage paysanne in lightly salted water for thirty seconds, drain and cool.
• Sear the scallops at high heat in an oiled skillet for one minute. Remove the scallops and keep warm.
• Add a little butter to the skillet and slowly sweat the shallots and the saffron.
• Deglaze with champagne and vermouth, reducing the sauce by three-quarters.
• Stir in the crayfish broth. Over high heat, further reduce the sauce by two-thirds.
• Heat the lobster meat and the scallops in the broth. When hot, remove and arrange on warmed plates.
• Reduce the broth by one-half, fold in the cabbage paysanne and remove from heat. Briskly whisk the softened butter into the hot sauce.
• Ladle the sauce over the stew. Garnish with the unbroken meat of the lobster claws.
• Serves 4. See photograph opposite this page.

Rendez-vous of Oysters and Calves' Brains 'Dom Perignon'

16 large oysters
⅔ lb calves' brains
1 cup softened butter
2 tbsp chopped shallots
*2 cups Dom Perignon**
1 ¼ cups 35% cream
⅛ cup leek paysanne
⅛ cup red pepper juliennes
salt, pepper

Shuck the oysters and wash them thoroughly.
• Place the brains in a bowl under cold running water for thirty minutes. Wash, trim and cut into small pieces.
• Blanch the leek paysanne and red pepper juliennes separately in lightly salted water. Keep warm.
• Butter a skillet and allow to brown lightly. Sauté the oysters and brains for one minute; remove from the pan and keep warm.
• Add a little butter to the pan and slowly sweat the shallots.
• Deglaze the pan with champagne and reduce the sauce by three-quarters.
• Stir in the cream. Further reduce the sauce until it coats the back of a wooden spoon. Remove from heat.
• Whisk the softened butter into the hot sauce.
• Centre the oysters and the brains on four warmed plates. Surround with the warm vegetables.
• Ladle the sauce generously over each portion. Serve immediately.
• Serves 4.

*Substitution: Any good champagne may be substituted for the Dom Perignon.

'He was a very valiant man who first adventured on eating of oysters!' *Thomas Fuller*

Salad Neptune

¾ lb large scallops
½ lb squid
12 jumbo shrimp
¼ cup salad shrimp
2 tbsp chopped shallots
4 garlic cloves, chopped
3 tsp fresh ginger root, chopped
⅓ cup virgin olive oil
1 ¼ cups dry white wine
⅓ cup lemon juice, freshly squeezed
3 sprigs fresh tarragon, chopped
black pepper, freshly ground
salt

The seafood:* Clean the scallops and the squid. Slice the squid in one inch rings. Peel and devein the jumbo shrimp.

• Heat the oil in a large skillet and sweat the garlic, shallots and chopped ginger over moderate heat.

• Add the seafood. Sauté briefly over high heat.

• Deglaze the pan with white wine and lemon juice.

• Bring the broth rapidly to the boil. Season with tarragon, salt and pepper.

• Remove from heat, cover, and chill in the refrigerator for at least two hours before serving.

½ head of radicchio
1 Belgian endive
1 head of Boston lettuce
olive oil
sherry vinegar
black pepper, freshly ground
salt

The salad: Prepare the greens thirty minutes before serving the salad. Clean and wash the greens; toss with olive oil and sherry vinegar.

• Arrange the greens on six plates to form a bed for the seafood. Sprinkle lightly with salt and pepper.

• Remove the chilled seafood from the refrigerator. Stir several times to mingle flavours before dividing into six portions. Arrange attractively on the prepared greens. Serve immediately.

• Serves 6.

*Freshness of the ingredients and a swift assembly are the critical factors in this salad. Select only the freshest of seafood, prepare all ingredients before beginning to assemble the salad, and work swiftly.

Shrimp with Soya Sauce and Ginger

24-28 large shrimps
3 tbsp chopped shallots
3 tbsp ginger root, chopped
⅓ cup dry white wine
2 oz champagne
soya sauce
⅓ cup 35% cream
⅓ cup softened butter
⅛ cup green onion juliennes

Lightly oil a cast-iron skillet. Sear the shrimps over very high heat for one minute; remove with a slotted spoon and keep warm.

• Add a little butter to the pan. Gently sweat the shallots and chopped ginger root for two minutes.

• Deglaze the pan with white wine and champagne. Reduce the sauce by two-thirds.

• Stir in the cream and further reduce the sauce until it coats the back of a wooden spoon.

• Remove the sauce from heat and whisk in the softened butter.

• Season to taste with soya sauce.

• Blanch the green onion juliennes, drain, and keep warm.

• Arrange six or seven shrimps in a circle on each plate, pointing tails to the centre. Overlap the shrimps slightly.

• Ladle the warm sauce over the shrimps and garnish with the green onion juliennes.

• Serves 4.

Fowl

Breast of Capon with Leek and Stilton
Chicken Quenelles on Morels and
Chanterelles
Chicken Ragoût *à la bourguignonne*
Chicken Thighs with Asparagus
and Crayfish
Confit of Duck
Grilled Pigeon with Whole Garlic Cloves
Roast Duck with Maple Syrup and Apples

Breast of Capon with Leek and Stilton

3 capon breasts
⅓ cup chicken stock (see page 11)
3 tsp chopped shallots
⅓ cup dry white wine
1 ¼ cups 35% cream
⅓ cup softened butter
*2 oz ripe stilton**
2 medium leeks, diced
salt, pepper
cayenne

Skin and debone the capon breasts. Cut in half.
• Heat chicken stock, white wine and shallots in a large pan. Bring to the boil.
• Poach the capon breasts in the stock for eight to ten minutes over low heat.
• Remove the breasts; keep them warm.
• Stir the cream into the stock and reduce the sauce by two-thirds.
• Add the stilton. Simmer the sauce until it coats the back of a wooden spoon.
• Turn the heat to low. Whisk in the softened butter, cover the sauce and keep it warm.
• Sauté the leeks in a little butter for five minutes over low heat.
• Distribute the leeks over six warmed plates. Place one capon breast on each serving of leeks, and spoon the sauce over the meat.
• Serves 6. See photograph opposite page 68.

*Be sure to use mature stilton for full flavour. The quantity of stilton may be increased to taste.

'Part of the secret of success in life is to eat what you like and let the food fight it out inside.'
Mark Twain

Chicken Quenelles on Morels and Chanterelles

1 cup chicken mousseline (see page 15)
2 ¼ cups chicken stock (see page 11)
*¾ cup chanterelles**
*½ cup morels**
3 tsp chopped shallots
⅓ cup softened butter
⅓ cup whipped cream
1 sprig rosemary, chopped
salt, pepper

Wash and slice the mushrooms.
• Bring the chicken stock to the boil, then lower to a gentle simmer. Use two spoons to form the mousseline into quenelles. Lay them carefully in the stock.
• Slowly simmer the quenelles for seven to nine minutes. Do not boil.
• Remove the quenelles, cover and keep warm.
• Reduce the chicken stock to one eighth.
• Gently sweat the shallots, mushrooms and rosemary in a little butter.
• Stir in the chicken stock and let the sauce simmer for two minutes.
• Remove the mushrooms with a slotted spoon. Turn off the heat under the sauce.
• Distribute the mushrooms evenly over four plates to form a bed for the quenelles. Distribute the quenelles. Keep the plates warm.
• Fold the whipped cream into the warmed sauce. Ladle the sauce over the quenelles and serve immediately.
• Decorate each serving with a sprig of rosemary.
• Serves 4.

*Substitution: Try Inoke, Oyster or Shiitake mushrooms; failing these, substitute button mushrooms.

Chicken Ragoût à la bourguignonne

2 chicken breasts
8 button mushrooms
1/8 cup chopped onion
1/8 cup carrot
1/8 cup celery root
1/8 cup rutabaga
1 chopped garlic clove
12 strips bacon
8 tbsp tomato paste
1/3 cup veal jus (see page 13)
1/3 cup chicken stock (see page 11)
1 1/4 cups red wine
1 sprig thyme, chopped
1 sprig rosemary, chopped
salt, pepper
paprika
flour

Cut the chicken breasts into half inch cubes. Quarter the mushrooms.
• Cut the root vegetables into quarter inch cubes and slice the bacon into juliennes.
• Season the chicken breasts with salt, pepper and paprika. Dust liberally with flour.
• Fry the bacon juliennes. Add the chicken and sauté until golden. Remove the chicken.
• Add a little butter to the pan. Slowly sweat the vegetables, tomato paste and herbs for five minutes.
• Stir the red wine into the sauce pan and reduce by one-half.
• Add the veal jus, chicken stock and the chicken breasts. Bring the sauce to the boil and simmer for thirty minutes, stirring occasionally.
• Serve on heated plates. Chop fresh thyme and rosemary and sprinkle over the chicken as a garnish.
• Serves 4.

Chicken Thighs with Asparagus and Crayfish

8 chicken thighs
12 crayfish
16 fresh green asparagus tips
1/3 cup softened butter
1 1/4 cups crayfish broth *(see page 12)*
1/3 cup champagne
1 1/4 cups 35% cream
salt, pepper
cayenne

Cook the asparagus tips in lightly salted water until crisp. Cool; slice the tips in half, length-wise.
• Cook the crayfish in lightly salted water. Cool; remove the tail meat.
• Season the chicken thighs with salt and pepper. Fry in a little butter for three minutes on each side.
• Add the champagne to the pan and reduce by half.
• Stir in the crayfish broth. Cover the pan and simmer the chicken for twenty minutes over medium heat.
• Remove the thighs and keep them warm.
• Stir in the cream, and further reduce the sauce until it coats the back of a wooden spoon. Season to taste. Remove from heat.
• Whisk in the softened butter. Place two chicken thighs on each of four warmed plates. Strain the sauce over the meat.
• Quickly sauté the asparagus and crayfish in a little butter. Season lightly and arrange attractively around the chicken.
• Serves 4.

Confit of Duck

1 three lb fresh duck, eviscerated
3/4 cup rock salt
6 crushed bay leaves
6 sprigs chopped thyme
8 sprigs chopped rosemary
1 chopped garlic clove
12 black peppercorns, crushed
4 cups duck fat

Make a marinade of the salt, bay leaves, thyme, rosemary, garlic and peppercorns.

• Remove the backbone of the duck. Quarter the duck, and rub each portion thoroughly with the marinade.

• Place the duck in a stone crock, skin up.

• Cover the duck and weight it. Refrigerate for two days.

• Melt the duck fat in a heavy pot. Wash the duck pieces, place them in the pot and simmer over low heat for two to three hours, or until tender.

• Remove the duck. Layer the pieces in the crock and allow to cool.

• Slowly drain the fat through a doubled cheesecloth into a sauce pan. Discard any juices that may have settled.

• Bring the fat to a simmer, skimming frequently to clarify.

• Pour the fat through a doubled cheesecloth onto the duck. Allow to cool. Refrigerate.

• To reheat, simply remove the layer of fat from the duck and place the duck on a rack in a large roasting pan. Bake at medium heat for ten minutes.

• Serve with your favourite chutney.

• Serves 4 to 6.

Note: This dish will mature and intensify in flavour with refrigeration. Well covered with fat, duck confit will keep in the refrigerator for up to six months.

Grilled Pigeon with Whole Garlic Cloves

4 plump young pigeons
16 garlic cloves, unpeeled
½ cup chicken stock (see page 11)
1 oz sherry
⅔ cup veal jus (see page 13)
2 tbsp softened butter
salt, pepper
paprika

Split the pigeons in half and remove the backbone. Lightly season inside and out with salt, pepper and paprika.

• Slowly roast the garlic cloves in a lightly buttered roasting pan until just brown.

• Stir in the sherry, and reduce the sauce to a minimum.

• Stir in the chicken stock and the veal jus. Simmer the garlic cloves in the sauce until tender; remove and reserve.

• Grill the pigeons on both sides, skin side first, for fifteen to twenty minutes at medium heat. Remove the breast bone. Cut each bird in half and place on a heated plate, one bird per serving.

• Reduce the sauce by two-thirds, seasoning to taste. Remove from heat and whisk in the softened butter.

• Add the garlic cloves to the sauce. Ladle the sauce generously over the pigeons.

• Serves 4.

Roast Duck with Maple Syrup and Apples

1 fresh duck, eviscerated
5 medium onions, sliced
2 large apples, peeled, cored and quartered
20 pecan halves
1/3 cup water
4 tbsp maple syrup
grated rind of 1 orange
1/3 cup softened butter
2 sprigs sage
salt, pepper
paprika

Preheat oven to 350°F.

• Remove the neck, wings and liver from the duck. Chop into hazelnut-sized pieces; line a large roasting pan with the chopped liver and bones.

• Stuff the duck with a quarter of the sliced onions, the sage sprigs, pecans and apple pieces. Tie the duck together.

• Place the duck on its back in the roasting pan. Add the water, maple syrup, and grated orange rind.

• Roast the duck in the oven for half an hour, basting every five minutes with the pan juices.

• Remove from the oven. Discard the fat; add the remaining onions to the pan. Put the duck back in the oven.

• Roast for another thirty to forty-five minutes, stirring the onions frequently. Remove from the oven; lift out the duck and place on a large platter. Keep warm.

• Skim the fat from the surface of the stock. Transfer the onions, bones and stock to a saucepan. Carefully drain the juices which have collected inside the duck, and add these to the saucepan.

• Reduce the stock by one-half. Fill the pan with cold water to the original level and reduce again by two-thirds.

• Force the sauce through a fine sieve into a second saucepan. Bring back to the boil.

• Remove from heat and whisk the softened butter into the hot sauce. Season to taste.

• Open the cooked duck, remove the backbone, and divide into four portions.

• Garnish each serving with apples and onions. Serve the sauce separately.

• Serves 4.

Meats

Beef Tenderloin 'Red Velvet'

2 lbs beef tenderloin (centre cut)*
salt, pepper
1 1/4 cups veal mousseline (see page 17)
6 large red cabbage leaves
1 1/4 cups vegetable broth (see page 14)

Preheat oven to 400°F.
• Season the tenderloin and sear both sides.
• Cut out and discard the core of a whole red cabbage. Submerge the cabbage briefly in boiling water to blanch the leaves; peel off the six largest leaves and allow to cool.
• Lay these leaves on a large square of tinfoil so that they overlap slightly.
• Spread a third of the veal mousseline in the centre of the cabbage leaves.
• Pat the tenderloin dry with paper towels. Place the meat on the bed of veal mousseline, covering it smoothly with the remaining mousseline.
• Carefully roll the edges of the tinfoil together to form a large sausage. Fold the edges to seal.
• Place the tinfoil sausage in a large roasting pan. Pour in the vegetable broth. Braise in the oven for forty-five minutes.
• Slice the tenderloin carefully. Serve with sauce hollandaise (see page 19).
• Serves 6.

Note: In 1985 I prepared this recipe at a gala dinner in Paris for the European press, substituting buffalo tenderloin for the beef tenderloin.

'Dinner, a time when ... one should eat wisely but not too well, and talk well but not too wisely!'
W. Somerset Maugham

Blanquette of Baby Goat with Morels

2 lbs baby goat meat
*1/2 cup fresh morels**
1/8 cup fresh peas
1 onion, spiked with 4 cloves
2 bay leaves
2/3 cup dry white wine
1 2/3 cups vegetable broth (see page 14)
1 cup 35% cream
salt, pepper

Clean and trim the goat meat, discarding the sinew and the membrane. Cut the meat into three-quarter inch cubes.
• Quarter the morels.
• Cook the peas in lightly salted water for thirty seconds. Immerse in ice-water to set colour; drain; reserve.
• Cook the goat meat in lightly salted water for one minute. Drain.
• Combine the goat meat with the white wine, the vegetable broth, the spiked onion and the bay leaves in a large pot. Bring rapidly to the boil. Reduce the heat to medium and simmer the meat, covered, for one hour.
• Remove the meat. Strain the stock through a doubled cheesecloth into a second pan. Add the cream and the morels. Slowly reduce the sauce by one-half.
• Add the goat meat. Simmer the blanquette for five more minutes.

1/3 cup 35% cream
4 egg yolks

The liaison: To form the liaison, mix the cream and egg yolks together. Turn off the heat under the blanquette and incorporate the liaison. Remove from the stove.
• Reheat the peas. Serve the blanquette on heated plates, garnished with the peas.
• Serves 6.

*Substitution: Substitute one-eighth cup dried morels. Presoak in cold water for one hour. Wash thoroughly, changing the water three times.

Braised Leg of Baby Goat with Rosemary

5 lb leg of baby goat
1/3 cup peanut oil
1/4 cup carrots
1/4 cup onion
1/8 cup celery root
15 sprigs rosemary, chopped
2 cups veal jus (see page 13)
2 cups dry white wine
1/8 cup butter
2 bay leaves
10 white peppercorns
salt, pepper

Preheat oven to 375°F.

• Clean the vegetables. Cut in half inch cubes.

• Trim the goat leg to fit the largest available roasting pan. If necessary, cut the leg in half at the hip joint.

• Rub the leg lightly with salt and pepper. Heat the peanut oil in a roasting pan on top of the stove, and roast the leg for three to four minutes on each side over medium heat.

• Remove the leg. Drain the oil from the pan.

• Add the butter to the pan. Roast the vegetables on top of the stove for five minutes.

• Add the rosemary, bay leaves and peppercorns. Roast for two more minutes.

• Stir in the veal jus and the white wine. Reduce the sauce by one-half.

• Replace the goat leg in the pan. Braise in the oven for one and a half to two hours, basting liberally with the sauce every ten minutes. Over this period the sauce will gradually reduce to a glaze. If necessary, dilute the glaze with a little cold water.

• Serves 10.

Braised Veal Shank à l'orange

3 lbs veal shank
1/4 cup unsalted butter
1/4 cup carrots
1/4 cup onions
1/4 cup celery heart
10 juicy oranges
1 1/4 cups maple syrup
2/3 cup white wine
2/3 cup veal jus
(see page 13)
1/3 cup vegetable broth
(see page 14)
salt, pepper
paprika

Preheat oven to 375°F.

• Clean the vegetables and cut them into half inch cubes.

• Trim the veal shank of excess fat or gristle; remove the membrane.

• Rub the shank lightly with salt, pepper and paprika.

• Melt the butter in a roasting pan on top of the stove. Slowly brown the shank all over.

• Remove the shank. Add the vegetables to the pan and roast them for five minutes over medium heat.

• Squeeze the oranges; grate the rinds of three. Add the juice and the gratings to the pan.

• Add the maple syrup, the white wine, the veal jus and the vegetable broth. Reduce the glaze by one-half.

• Put the shank back in the pan and baste well. Braise slowly in the oven for one and a half hours, basting liberally with the glaze every ten minutes.

• Serves 6.

Grilled Rabbit Loins with Pommery Mustard and Pistachios

8 rabbit loins
peanut oil
salt, pepper

Remove the membranes from the rabbit loins and baste them with peanut oil.
• While making the sauce, grill the loins until medium rare.

1 tbsp chopped shallots
3 tbsp pistachios, peeled and chopped
2 tbsp pommery mustard
1/3 cup white wine
2/3 cup veal jus *(see page 13)*
1 cup 35% cream
1/8 cup softened butter
chopped parsley

The sauce: Butter a saucepan lightly. Sweat the shallots and pistachios for two minutes on medium heat.
• Stir in the white wine and the veal jus. Reduce the sauce by one-half.
• Stir in the cream and the pommery mustard. Reduce the sauce until it coats the back of a wooden spoon. Turn down the heat.
• Slice the grilled loins.
• Ladle the sauce onto four heated plates. Place two rabbit loins on each plate in the centre of the sauce.
• Serves 4. See photograph opposite page 69.

Poached Beef Tenderloin with Horseradish and Mint

6 five oz beef tenderloins
4 cups vegetable broth (see page 14)

Bring the vegetable broth to the boil. Poach the beef tenderloins until medium rare.
• Remove the tenderloins, cover and keep warm.

1 ⅔ cups 35% cream
*3 tsp grated horseradish**
6 sprigs mint leaves, chopped
⅛ cup softened butter
salt, pepper

The sauce: Reduce the vegetable broth over very high heat to one eighth of the original quantity.
• Stir in the cream and the horseradish. Reduce until the sauce coats the back of a wooden spoon.
• Whisk the softened butter into the sauce. Fold in the chopped mint leaves. Season to taste.
• Ladle the sauce onto six heated plates.
• Slice each tenderloin into four thin slices and centre on the sauce.
• Garnish with mint sprigs.
Serves 6. See photograph opposite this page.

*Substitution: The quantity cited is based on bottled horseradish. Halve the quantity for fresh horseradish, which is considerably sharper.

Pork Tenderloin with Dijon Mustard and Honey

6 five oz
pork tenderloins
peanut oil
salt, pepper

Season the tenderloins. Fry in a skillet over moderate heat, turning the loins until medium rare on both sides.

- Remove the loins, cover and keep warm.

3 tsp chopped shallots
2 oz dry vermouth
1/3 cup white wine
2/3 cup veal jus
(see page 13)
4 tbsp dark honey
3 tsp dijon mustard
1 1/4 cups 35% cream
1/4cup softened butter
chopped parsley
salt, pepper

The sauce: Melt a little butter in the same pan. Sweat the shallots for two minutes over medium heat.

- Stir in the vermouth, the white wine and the veal jus. Reduce the sauce by one-half.
- Fold in the honey and the cream; reduce by half again.
- Whisk in the dijon mustard and bring the sauce to a rapid boil. Turn off the heat.
- Whisk the softened butter into the hot sauce. Season with salt and pepper.
- Slice the pork tenderloins.
- Mix the chopped parsley into the sauce and spoon onto heated plates. Serve each sliced tenderloin on the warm sauce.
- Serves 6. See photograph opposite this page.

Roast Stuffed Saddle of Lamb

8 lb saddle of lamb
¾ cup chicken mousseline (see page 15)
⅛ cup carrot
⅛ cup kohlrabi, or turnip
⅛ cup celery
3 tsp peas
⅛ cup small green beans
pig's caul
⅓ cup vegetable oil

Preheat oven to 375°F.
• Peel and debone the lamb saddle, leaving the back intact. Chop the bones into hazelnut-sized pieces.
• Clean the vegetables and cut into eighth-inch cubes. Blanch each vegetable in a separate pot for thirty seconds: the water should be lightly salted. Immerse in ice-water to cool. Drain.
• Combine the vegetables and the chicken mousseline, mixing well.
• Wash the pig's caul. Spread sufficient quantity to cover the entire lamb saddle onto a cheesecloth.
• Lay the saddle on the cheesecloth, back down. Fill the saddle with the mousseline/vegetable mixture.
• Fold the saddle together. Tie firmly, so that the pig's caul completely envelops the folded saddle. Heat oil in a large roasting pan until it sizzles. Place the wrapped saddle in the pan, back up.
• Roast in the oven for one and a half hours, basting with oil every fifteen minutes. Remove, unwrap, and slice the saddle.

½ lb lamb bones
4 tbsp tomato paste
¾ cup vegetable broth (see page 14)
¾ cup veal jus (see page 13)
¾ cup white wine
¼ cup softened butter
3 sprigs thyme
salt, pepper

The sauce: Heat a little oil in a large skillet.
• Roast the lamb bones slowly.
• Add the thyme and the tomato paste. Simmer for fifteen to twenty minutes, stirring constantly.
• Stir in the white wine in two stages, reducing the sauce after each addition.
• Add the veal jus and the vegetable broth, further reducing the sauce to one third.
• Strain the sauce through a cheesecloth into a second pan. Bring the sauce back to the boil, turn off the heat and quickly whisk in the softened butter.
• Serve the sliced saddle on the sauce.
• Serves 6 to 8.

Roast Veal Loin with Chantarelles

2 lbs veal loin
vegetable oil
3 tbsp chopped shallots
8 oz chanterelles, washed and sliced
⅓ cup softened butter
⅓ cup white wine
⅓ cup veal jus (see page 13)
1 ¼ cups 35% cream
salt, pepper

Preheat oven to 375°F.

• Remove any membranes from the veal loin. Season. Sear on both sides in a lightly oiled skillet.

• Roast the loin in the oven for twenty to twenty-five minutes. Remove, cover and keep warm.

• Melt a little butter in the same pan. Sweat the shallots and the chanterelles for three minutes over medium heat.

• Add the white wine and the veal jus. Slowly reduce the sauce by one-half.

• Add the cream and any juices from the roasted loin. Reduce the sauce until it coats the back of a wooden spoon.

• Season to taste. Remove from heat and whisk in the softened butter.

• Reheat the veal loin in a hot oven for five minutes. Slice thinly. Serve in a pool of warm sauce on heated plates.

• Serves 6.

Sautéed Lamb Loins with Ginger and Chives

*6 five oz lamb loins**
peanut oil
salt, pepper

Trim the loins of excess fat and gristle. Season with salt and pepper.

• Heat the peanut oil in a large skillet. Fry the loins on both sides until medium rare. Remove and keep warm.

3 tsp chopped shallots
3 tsp ginger root, chopped
1/3 cup white wine
2/3 cup veal jus (see page 13)
2/3 cup lamb jus (see page 13)
1/8 cup softened butter
chopped chives
salt, pepper

The sauce: Drain the skillet and discard the fat. Add a little butter and gently sweat the shallots and the ginger root for two minutes.

• Stir in the white wine and the veal jus. Reduce by two-thirds.

• Add the lamb sauce and the chives. Boil for two minutes. Turn off the heat.

• Whisk the softened butter into the hot sauce. Season with salt and pepper.

To serve: Slice the warm lamb loins. Ladle the sauce onto six heated plates and present each loin in the centre of the sauce.

• Serves 6. See photograph opposite page 88.

*Select fresh Canadian (or American) lamb when available. New Zealand lamb tends to be smaller: two loins per serving may be necessary.

Tournedos with Black Cherries and Green Peppercorns

6 five oz beef tournedos
peanut oil
salt, pepper

Season the meat well. Heat the peanut oil in a large skillet. Fry the tournedos over moderate heat until both sides are medium rare.

• Remove from the pan, cover and keep warm.

3 tsp chopped shallots
2 tsp green peppercorns
1/8 cup sour black cherries
1/3 cup port wine
1 2/3 cups veal jus (see page 13)
1/3 cup 35% cream
1/4 cup softened butter
salt

The sauce: Add a little butter to the skillet. Sweat the shallots and the peppercorns until the peppercorns burst.

• Add the cherries and the port wine. Reduce by half.

• Stir in the veal jus, and over high heat again reduce the sauce by half.

• Add the cream and reduce by half. Remove from heat and whisk in the softened butter.

Season with salt. Serve the tournedos on the warm sauce on heated plates.

• Serves 6.

'A slice of a cow's rear is very valuable to a cow, but it is worth only a dime to a farmer, twenty-five cents to a meat packer, fifty-six cents to a retail butcher and a dollar and fifty cents to a restaurant, not counting the tip and side dishes.' *Andy Clarke* (1949)

Tripe in Champagne with Asparagus

*1 1/3 lbs tripe**
4 cups water
1/4 cup vinegar
1 tbsp unsalted butter
salt

Clean the tripe. Cook in salted vinegar-water for twenty minutes. Allow to cool.

• When cool, drain the tripe and slice in one-third inch strips.

• Brown one tbsp of butter in a skillet. Fry the tripe for two minutes. Season with salt and pepper and distribute over four heated plates. Keep warm.

16 green asparagus tips
1/8 cup carrot juliennes
2 cups champagne
2/3 cup veal jus (see page 13)
2/3 cup whipped cream
chopped parsley
salt, pepper

The sauce: Barely cover the asparagus tips with lightly salted water and cook for two minutes. Remove with a slotted spoon; cool, slice in half length-wise.

• In the asparagus-water cook the carrot juliennes for one minute. Remove with a slotted spoon, reserve.

• Add the champagne to the vegetable water. Reduce to one-third cup.

• Add the veal jus, and reduce again by half. Season to taste.

• Mix the asparagus tips, carrot juliennes and chopped parsley into the sauce. Fold in the whipped cream.

• Ladle the sauce over the tripe and serve immediately.

• Serves 4.

*Use calf's tripe for this recipe. Beef tripe require lengthy stewing to be edible.

Veal Paupiettes with Sage

12 two oz veal medallions
1 1/2 cups veal mousseline (see page 17)
2 tsp chopped shallots
1/3 cup madeira
1/3 cup red wine
1 2/3 cups veal jus (see page 13)
4 sprigs sage leaves, chopped
1/4 cup softened butter
salt, pepper
olive oil

Preheat oven to 400°F.
• Place the medallions between two sheets of plastic wrap and pound until very thin.
• Season the medallions with salt and pepper on both sides. Top each medallion with a dollop of mousseline.
• Fold the medallion in on itself at either end, then roll lengthwise to form a paupiette. Secure with a toothpick.
• Heat a little olive oil in a skillet. Fry the paupiettes until lightly brown all over.
• Transfer the skillet to the hot oven. Roast the paupiettes for fifteen to twenty minutes, turning occasionally.
• Remove the skillet. Transfer the paupiettes to another pan, cover, and keep warm.
• Melt a little butter in the hot skillet. Sweat the shallots for two minutes over medium heat, adding the chopped sage leaves for the last thirty seconds.
• Pour in the madeira and the red wine. Reduce the sauce to half the original quantity.
• Add the veal jus and reduce the sauce to three-quarters of a cup.
• Strain the sauce through a cheesecloth into a second pan. Bring back to the boil; turn off the heat.
• Whisk the softened butter into the hot sauce. Season to taste.
• Arrange the paupiettes on six warmed plates, two paupiettes per serving.
• Serve immediately.
• Serves 6. See photograph opposite this page.

Note: Delicious with potato gnocchi! (See page 99.)

Veal Sweetbreads with Anchovies and Olives

1 ¼ lbs veal sweetbreads
1 oz olive oil
1 tbsp butter, unsalted
salt, pepper
flour

The meat: Soak the sweetbreads under cold running water for two hours. Remove the skin, fat, and blood vessels.
• Slice the sweetbreads into two-third inch medallions. Season the sweetbreads and dust lightly with flour. Melt the butter with olive oil in a skillet. Fry the medallions for four to five minutes on each side. Keep warm.

4 chopped anchovies
12 stuffed olives, chopped
⅓ cup white wine
⅔ cup veal jus (see page 13)
lemon juice
2 tbsp softened butter
chopped chervil
salt, pepper

The sauce: Sweat the anchovies, olives and shallots in a little butter for one minute.
• Deglaze the pan with the white wine and the veal jus. Reduce the sauce by one-half.
• Season with lemon juice, salt and pepper. Add the chopped chervil and turn off the heat. Whisk the softened butter into the hot sauce.
• Serve the sweetbreads in a bed of sauce on warmed plates. Garnish with chervil leaves.
• Serves 4.

Vegetables

Asparagus Milanaise
with Quail Eggs and Thyme
Boulangère Potatoes
Braised Fennel
Braised Red Cabbage
Champagne Sauerkraut
Gratin Monégasque
Potato Gnocchi with Thyme
Potato Gratin
Ratatouille
Rösti Potatoes
Vichy Carrots

*Asparagus Milanaise with Quail Eggs and Thyme**

24 green asparagus, peeled
8 quail eggs
3 tbsp grated parmesan
5/8 cup unsalted butter
1/8 cup 35% cream
salt, pepper
thyme leaves

Cut the asparagus stalks into one inch pieces, slicing on an angle. Discard the ends. Reserve whole tips intact.

• Blanch stalks and tips separately in lightly salted water. Immerse in an ice-water bath to cool and set the colour.

• Sauté the asparagus stalks in a little butter for thirty seconds. Then add the cream and thyme leaves. Reduce the cream quickly over high heat. When the ragoût has thickened nicely, turn down the heat. Keep warm.

• Break the quail eggs carefully into a lightly buttered teflon pan. Fry the eggs gently, sunny-side up.

• Reheat the blanched asparagus tips and arrange them in fan shapes on four plates. Spoon the ragoût generously over the tips.

• Sprinkle with grated parmesan and gratinée quickly.

• Just before serving, centre two fried quail eggs on each portion, surrounded by the ragoût. Serve immediately.

• Serves 4.

*Serve as a vegetable or as an appetizer.

'Cuisine is when things taste like themselves.'
Maurice Edmond Sailland ('Curnonsky')

Boulangère Potatoes

8 large potatoes, peeled
1 large onion, peeled
1/4 cup unsalted butter
1/3 cup peanut oil
salt, pepper

Slice the potatoes into one-eighth inch slices and blanch them for one minute in lightly salted water. Drain and pat dry.

• Melt the butter in a small skillet. Slice the onion finely and sweat in the butter over medium heat until nicely brown and carmelized.

• Heat the peanut oil in a large skillet. Fry the potatoes in the oil until golden brown on both sides.

• Carefully work in the onions, slipping them under the potatoes.

• Fry for one more minute, and season to taste.

• Serves 4.

Braised Fennel

3 large fennel
1/4 cup diced carrot
1/4 cup diced onion
1/8 cup diced celery
8 strips bacon
1/4 cup chicken stock (see page 11)
salt, pepper

Preheat oven to 350°F.

• Wash the fennel thoroughly to remove sand. Cut off the fern, discard the two large outer leaves and slice the stalks in half length-wise.

• Sauté the bacon and the remaining vegetables in a large skillet for five minutes over medium heat.

• Transfer the sautéed vegetables to a ovenproof casserole. Place the fennel on top of the vegetables, with the cut surface facing down.

• Add the chicken stock and bring to the boil. Cover the casserole and braise in the oven for one hour, or until soft.

• Remove from the oven. Cut out the fennel cores and discard. Slice the fennel stalks in large slices. Serve with fresh tomato sauce (see page 18) or sprinkle with grated parmesan and gratinée briefly.

• Serves 6.

Braised Red Cabbage

1 red cabbage, shredded
¾ cup red wine vinegar
2 cups red wine
⅓ cup fresh orange juice
1 large onion, chopped
⅓ cup goose or pork fat
6 Golden Delicious apples
salt, pepper
cinnamon
sugar

Mix the shredded cabbage with salt, sugar and vinegar. Marinate for twenty-four hours.

• Melt the fat in an ovenproof casserole. Sweat the onions in the fat for ten minutes. Add the marinated cabbage, the marinade and the red wine.

• Cover the casserole and simmer in a medium oven for two hours.

• Peel and core the apples and cut them into thin slices.

• Add the orange juice and apple slices to the cabbage. Bake uncovered for an additional thirty minutes, stirring occasionally.

• Season to taste with salt, pepper, sugar and cinnamon.

• Serves 8 to 10.

Champagne Sauerkraut

1 ½ cups sauerkraut
2 onions, sliced
6 carrots, grated
2 garlic cloves, chopped
5 tart apples, grated
4 sprigs thyme
2 whole cloves
8 juniper berries
2 bay leaves
1 smoked pork hock
salt, pepper
1 bottle champagne (brut)
⅓ cup goose fat
⅓ cup 35% cream

Preheat oven to 300°F.

• Wash the sauerkraut thoroughly. Drain.

• Melt the goose fat in a large skillet. Sauté the remaining vegetables and seasonings slowly over low heat for ten minutes. Transfer the vegetables to an ovenproof casserole and sprinkle with the grated apple.

• Cut the pork hock in half. Place both portions on top of the vegetables, cut surface down.

• Cover with the sauerkraut and drench with champagne.

• Cover the casserole and bake in the oven until the meat is cooked to the bone.

• Continue to bake until most of the liquid has evaporated. Remove from heat, fold in the cream and serve.

• Serves 8.

Gratin Monégasque

2 large zucchini
1 medium eggplant
4 large tomatoes, peeled
6 tbsp olive oil
chopped oregano
chopped thyme
1/8 cup grated gruyère
3 tbsp grated parmesan
salt, pepper

Preheat oven to 350°F.
• Slice the vegetables thinly. Arrange them in alternate layers on a buttered, ovenproof casserole.
• Sprinkle liberally with the olive oil and the fresh herbs. Season with salt and pepper.
• Cover with the grated cheese and bake in the oven for forty minutes.
• If necessary, cover the casserole with tin foil to prevent burning.
• Serves 4.

Potato Gnocchi with Thyme

8 large, starchy potatoes
1 2/3 cup flour
1/3 cup semolina
3 egg yolks
salt
nutmeg
1/3 cup grated parmesan
1/3 cup unsalted butter
8 sprigs chopped thyme

Wash the potatoes. Cook in salted water until tender; drain and peel. Force the hot potatoes through a fine sieve or ricer.

• Cool. Add the flour, semolina, egg yolks and chopped thyme to the potatoes. Work quickly together into a dough, blending well. Season to taste.

• Roll the dough into finger-thick rolls. Slice into half-inch pieces. Dust lightly with flour. Press each piece of dough gently with a floured fork.

• Simmer the gnocchi in salted water for four minutes. Drain carefully and transfer to a buttered ovenproof casserole.

• Sprinkle with parmesan cheese and gratinée quickly.

• Heat the butter in a small skillet until lightly browned. Stir in the chopped thyme leaves. Pour the herbed butter over the gnocchi.

• Serves 6.

Note: Gnocchi are delicious doused with tomato sauce (see page 18) and served as an appetizer.

Potato Gratin

8 large potatoes
1 1/4 cups milk
3/4 cup 35% cream
2 garlic cloves
1/8 cup butter
salt, pepper
nutmeg
1/3 cup gruyère cheese

Preheat oven to 350°F.

• Peel the potatoes and slice them thinly. (Do not wash the potatoes: washing removes some of the starch.)

• Mince the garlic and mix with the potatoes.

• Combine the milk and potatoes in an iron casserole. Season to taste with salt, pepper and grated nutmeg.

• Bring to the boil over high heat until the starch of the potatoes has slightly thickened the milk. Then add half the cream; re-season; bring back to the boil. Remove from heat.

• Butter a shallow ovenproof casserole and arrange the potatoes in a one inch layer.

• Fold the remaining cream gently under the potatoes.

• Cook in the oven for approximately one hour.

• Sprinkle the gratin with grated gruyère cheese and dot with butter. Gratinée under the broiler.

• Serves 6 to 8.

Ratatouille

4 tomatoes, peeled and seeded
1 red pepper
1 green pepper
2 medium zucchini
½ eggplant
¼ English cucumber
4 tbsp tomato paste
⅓ cup chicken stock (see page 11)
⅓ cup olive oil
chopped oregano
chopped thyme
¼ cup grated gruyère
3 tbsp grated parmesan
⅛ cup unsalted butter
salt, pepper

Preheat oven to 425°F.
• Clean the vegetables and cut them into one inch cubes.
• Heat the olive oil in a skillet. Sauté the vegetables for five minutes over medium heat.
• Stir in the tomato paste and the herbs, mixing thoroughly.
• Add the chicken stock and simmer for one minute. Season to taste.
• Transfer the ratatouille to an ovenproof casserole. Sprinkle with grated cheese and dot with butter. Bake for ten minutes, or until the cheese melts.
• Serves 6 to 8.

Rösti Potatoes

8 large potatoes, unpeeled
1/8 cup bacon juliennes
4 tbsp chopped onion
1/4 cup unsalted butter
1 tsp cumin seed
salt, pepper
chopped parsley

Brush the potatoes. Boil them in water with cumin seed until tender (ten to fifteen minutes). Allow to cool.

• Peel the potatoes and grate them coarsely in long strips.

• Sauté the bacon and onion together until the onions are transparent. Reserve.

• Lightly brown the butter in a teflon pan. Spread half of the potato strips evenly over the pan; sprinkle with the onion-bacon mixture.

• Spread the remaining potato strips on top, pressing lightly. Season with salt and pepper.

• Sauté both sides, flipping the potato mixture like a pancake.

• When both sides are golden, lever the pancake onto a platter. Sprinkle with chopped parsley. To serve, cut in wedges.

• Serves 6.

Vichy Carrots

8 carrots
1/8 cup softened butter
chopped parsley
chopped chervil
salt, sugar, water

Peel the carrots and cut them into thin, uniform slices. Sweat in one tbsp of butter for three minutes.
• Season with salt and sugar. Cover with a minimum of water.
• Cover the pan and simmer the carrots slowly. Immediately before serving fold in the remaining softened butter.
• Sprinkle with chopped parsley and chervil. Present on warmed plates or in a bowl.
• Serves 6.

Desserts

Alsatian Plum Tart
Caledon Apple Tart
Champagne Tarragon Sherbet
Chocolate Mousse with Armagnac
Espresso Ice-Cream
Ginger Cranberry Sherbet
Old-Fashioned Plum Pudding
Orange and Port Sabayon
Peppered Strawberries
Wild Strawberry Foam

Alsatian Plum Tart

9 cups all-purpose flour
1 3/4 cups butter, unsalted
1 1/4 tbsp sugar
3 3/4 cups cold water

The dough (pâté brisée):* Work the butter into the flour by hand. Form a well in the centre of the dough.
• Pour the sugar and the water into the well. Incorporate quickly.
• Wrap the dough securely and refrigerate for two hours.

3/4 lb pâté brisée
3 lbs prune plums
3 tbsp Armagnac
12 tbsp graham cracker crumbs
8 tbsp hazelnuts, ground
1 tbsp white sugar
1 tsp icing sugar

The tart: Roll out the dough on a lightly floured surface to form a circle one-eighth inch thick. Drape over the rolling pin and lower the dough into a nine inch flan. (The pan should have a removeable fluted rim.)
• Press the dough firmly into the pan, allowing a three-eighth inch margin. Press the margin against the rim to from a fluted edge.
• Prick the pastry shell with a fork and refrigerate for one hour. Preheat oven to 450°F.
• Wash, pit, and halve the plums. Slice each plum-half in half again, just to the mid-point. (This creates the effect of two leaves joined at the base.)
• Marinate the plums with the Armagnac in the refrigerator for one hour, tossing occasionally. Drain, reserving the marinade.
• Mix the cracker crumbs and ground hazelnuts with the marinade. Sprinkle the bottom of the pastry shell with this mixture. Arrange the plums upright in the pastry shell, skin side outward, in a circular pattern.
• Mix the sugars together and dust the plums. Bake the tart for one hour.
• Allow the tart to cool briefly. Dust with icing sugar. Serve with whipped cream.
• Serves 8.

*This recipe makes enough dough for four to five tarts. To store, divide into four or five portions, wrap securely in plastic and freeze.

Caledon Apple Tart

4 cups all-purpose flour
14 tbsp butter
1 egg yolk
2/3 cup water
2 tsp salt
1 tsp white vinegar

The pastry: Preheat oven to 400°F.

• Rub flour and butter together thoroughly. Add the egg yolk, water, vinegar and salt and work the dough into a ball. Refrigerate in plastic wrap for one hour.

• On a lightly floured surface, roll out the dough to fit a nine inch flan. (Choose a pan with a removable fluted rim.) When the pastry is an eighth of an inch thick, drape it carefully over the rolling pin and lower into the flan. Press firmly. Prick the bottom with a fork.

• Bake at 400°F. for approximately thirty minutes. (To prevent excessive shrinking line the pastry with waxed or parchment paper, one inch larger than the flan and fill the cavity with dried lentils. After pre-baking, remove paper and lentils.) While the pastry is baking, prepare the filling.

1/2 cup milk
1/2 cup sour cream
1 egg
3 tsp flour
2 1/2 tbsp sugar
grated rind of 1 lemon
vanilla
8 tart apples, peeled and sliced

The custard: Whisk the sugar with the egg. Gradually add the milk, sour cream, flour, lemon rind and vanilla, whisking constantly.

• Line the pie shell with apple slices, overlapping the slices to completely cover the pastry.

• Pour the custard over the apple slices. Bake for thirty-five to forty minutes at 300°F..

• Serves 6 to 8.

'How long does getting thin take?'
Winnie the Pooh

Champagne Tarragon Sherbet

2 ¼ cups sugar
4 cups water
3 tsp chopped tarragon
6 cups champagne
juice of 1 lemon
3 egg whites

Combine the sugar, water, and tarragon in a large pan. Bring to the boil.

• Add the champagne and the lemon juice.

• Freeze the sherbet in an ice-cream machine for thirty minutes.

• Beat three egg whites until stiff and fold into the sherbet, one at a time. Return to the freezer for a final half-hour.

• Serves 15 to 20 as a palate refresher, or 10 people as a summer dessert.

Chocolate Mousse with Armagnac

1 cup milk
1/4 cup 35% cream
1 egg
1/8 cup sugar
3 tsp cornstarch
*10 oz dark chocolate**
1 tbsp powdered gelatin†
2 tbsp Armagnac
1 cup whipped cream

Soak the gelatine in a little water for five minutes.
• Bring the milk, cream and sugar to the boil in a large pan.
• Combine the cornstarch, egg, and a few drops of cold milk in a stainless steel bowl. Whisk thoroughly.
• Stir the cornstarch mixture into the boiling milk. Stir vigorously for at least three minutes at a brisk boil.
• Add the chocolate pieces and allow to melt into the hot milk.
• Add the gelatin. Stir well.
• Pour in the Armagnac. Remove from heat and whip briskly until the mixture is barely lukewarm.
• When the mousse is quite cool, carefully fold in the whipped cream with a spatula.
• Fill a one quart mold with the mousse. Refrigerate for a minimum of three hours.
• Serves 8 to 10.

*Use either Belgian or Swiss semi-sweet chocolate.

† Substitution: 6-7 gelatin leaves (available in European delis).

Espresso Ice-Cream

4 cups milk
4 cups 35% cream
14 egg yolks
2 cups sugar
*2 double espresso**

Blend the milk with the cream. Bring to the boil.
• Mix the egg yolks and sugar thoroughly together. Whisk briskly into the hot milk.
• Continue to boil for three minutes, whisking constantly.
• Allow to cool. Prepare two double espressos and mix with the cooled custard. Freeze in an ice-cream machine for an hour.
• Serves 15 to 20.

Variation: Chocolate ice-cream: melt ten oz of baker's semi-sweet chocolate. Add to the cooled custard, mix well and freeze.

*This recipe calls for about 1 ½ cups of espresso coffee, brewed at double strength in an espresso-maker. For a stronger flavour, increase the quantity of espresso.

Ginger Cranberry Sherbet

1 ¼ cups water
¾ cup white wine
1 ¾ cups white sugar
2 cups fresh cranberries
1 tbsp ginger root, chopped
candied ginger

Combine the water, white wine and sugar in a large pan. Bring to the boil.

• Wash the cranberries. Add with the chopped ginger to the hot syrup. Cover.

• Cook for five to seven minutes, or until the berries have burst.

• Allow the berries to cool in the syrup. Purée in a blender or food processor.

• Strain the syrup through a fine sieve, pressing the berries with the back of a metal spoon.

• Chill the syrup. Freeze in an ice-cream machine for a minimum of one hour.

• Garnish with candied ginger.

• Serves 15 as a palate refresher, or 8 to 10 as a dessert.

*Old-Fashioned Plum Pudding**

4 slices white bread
1 1/4 cups milk
1 tbsp beef suet
3 tbsp brown sugar
1 egg
1 1/4 cups orange juice
1/8 cup golden raisins
1/8 cup chopped dates
2 tbsp chopped walnuts
2 tbsp chopped pecans
3/4 cup all-purpose flour
1 1/4 tsp cinnamon
1/2 tsp ground clove
1/2 tsp mace
1 1/2 tsp baking powder
1 1/2 cups malt whiskey

Soften the bread in the milk. Break into small pieces.
• Add the brown sugar, suet, orange juice and egg.
• Mix in the raisins, chopped dates and chopped nuts. Blend well.
• Mix the flour and baking powder with the spices. Blend well with the fruit mixture.
• Pour in the whiskey. Mix the entire pudding very thoroughly.
• Fill a greased bowl with the pudding, wrap with cheesecloth, cover and steam over a double boiler for four and a half hours.
• To serve, invert the bowl onto a plate. Serve with hard sauce.
• Serves 10.

*Prepare this pudding one year in advance. Wrap well and store in a cool place.

Orange and Port Sabayon

¾ cup white wine
4 tbsp port
4 tbsp white sugar
*4 tsp orange juice**
zest of 1 orange
5 egg yolks
4 tsp Grand Marnier

Combine the wine, port, Grand Marnier, sugar, orange juice and zest. Let sit for thirty minutes.
• Strain through a cheesecloth into a stainless steel bowl.
• Place the bowl above a double boiler and over rapidly boiling water whisk in the egg yolks, beating constantly until the sabayon is thick and creamy. Quantity should double in volume.
• Serve the sabayon warm or chilled in tall glasses, garnished with mint. Delicious poured warm over fresh strawberries.
• Serves 5 to 6.

*Seville or blood oranges are ideal.

Peppered Strawberries

6 cups strawberries
2 1/2 tbsp white sugar
2 tbsp Kirsch
2 tbsp Grand Marnier
4 large scoops strawberry ice-cream
2/3 cup 35% cream, whipped
black pepper, freshly ground

Hull, wash and quarter the strawberries.
• Mix the strawberries with the sugar, Kirsch and Grand Marnier. Marinate for fifteen minutes.
• Dust the berries generously with black pepper, grinding the pepper mill twenty-five times.
• Whisk the strawberry ice-cream in a wooden bowl until soft. Fold in the whipped cream.
• Add the berries and their marinade. Mix carefully.
• Serve in glass bowls or tall glasses. Garnish each serving with a mint leaf.
• Serves 6.

Wild Strawberry Foam

3 egg yolks
1 ¼ cups wild strawberries
⅓ cup white sugar
½ lemon, juiced
1 cup 35% cream, whipped

Hull and wash the strawberries.
• Cover the strawberries with the lemon juice and half the sugar. Bring to a boil, simmer briefly and cool.
• Purée in a blender or food processor and reserve. Over rapidly boiling water, whisk the egg yolks with the rest of the sugar to a stiff foam.
• Add the puréed strawberry mixture to the foam and gently fold in the whipped cream.
• Distribute the mousse among four molds. Freeze for a minimum of three hours.

1 ⅔ cups wild strawberries
¼ cup white sugar

The sauce: Simmer one and two-thirds cups wild strawberries and a quarter cup sugar together briefly. Chill this sauce.
• To serve, unmold each mousse onto a chilled plate. Cover with the cold sauce and garnish with mint leaves.
• Serves 4.

'Desserts ... remain for a moment in your mouth and for the rest of your life on your hips.'
Peg Bracken

About the Author

Three summer seasons at the Grand Hotel National, Luzern, Switzerland; two winter seasons at the Derby Hotel, Davos, Switzerland.

• Began apprenticeship at age fifteen; my interest in this profession was sparked by my parents who both have a natural flair and interest in fine cooking.

• In Europe, studying and learning the fine art of cooking is an established and honorable profession and to enter this field is not as unusual as it is in Canada.

• Fortunately, I was lucky enough to be accepted into one of the most prestigious grand hotels in Europe for my apprenticeship.

• The Grand Hotel National in Luzern, where Auguste Escoffier once worked still enjoys a reputation of being one of the grand luxury hotels. It was here, under the guidance of Chef de Cuisine Gustav Partsch, that I acquired my knowledge of classical cuisine.

• Throughout my three years of schooling, I was also tutored periodically by Anton Mosimann, who is now Executive Chef of the Dorchester Hotel, London, England and is regarded as one of the great chefs in Europe today.

• Graduated at the top of my class of 250 apprentices in 1976 and received my chef's papers certified by the Swiss Government.

• It was Dante Rota, Chef-Patron of 'Noodles' Restaurant in Toronto, who allowed me to develop and implement my culinary abilities while working for him at the Windsor Arms Hotel. He also helped me to develop administrative skills, which are essential, but unfortunately require too much valuable time.

• Upon graduation in 1976, I was fortunate to join the Hotel Waldhaus Dolder, Zurich, Switzerland, as

Commis Tournant.

• In 1977 I accepted the position of Chef Entremetier, at the Restaurant Schützenhaus, Basel, Switzerland.

• I came to the Banff Springs Hotel, Banff, Alberta, in the spring of 1978 on a one year work permit. Both the Executive Chef and the Executive Sous Chef at the Banff Springs Hotel were from my hometown in Switzerland.

• I met my future wife, Tara, a Canadian girl, a short time later, and decided to make Canada my home. We now have two children, Erika and Hedy.

• From 1981 to 1983 I was Assistant Executive Chef at the Windsor Arms Hotel, Toronto, Ontario.

• In 1984 I was delighted to accept my current position of Chef de Cuisine at The Millcroft Inn, Alton, Ontario.

Helpful Hints

Butter: For fine cooking, use only unsalted butter. Since salt acts as a preservative, salted butter has the advantage of keeping longer, but in cooking it is a poor substitute for unsalted or fresh sweet butter.

Softened butter and hot sauces: Many recipes in this collection call for the addition of softened butter. This is butter that has been removed from the refrigerator and allowed to soften to room temperature, but not to liquefy. Butter with an oily gleam should be returned to the refrigerator.

When adding butter to a hot sauce the temperature of the sauce is critical. If the sauce is too hot, or actually boiling, the butter will 'break' – separate into fat and buttermilk – and ruin the texture of the sauce. If the sauce is too cool the butter will not melt satisfactorily, leaving persistent little lumps throughout the sauce. For this reason recipe instructions specify that the heat under the saucepan must be turned off, or the pan removed from the heat, before the softened butter is whisked into the sauce. Serve promptly.

Measurements: The measurements in this book relate to the ingredients I use in The Millcroft Inn kitchen. These measurements are strictly guidelines and a recipe may turn out differently from time to time, according to the ingredients you buy. If the recipe calls, however, for two tablespoons of chopped parsley, and you have only one tablespoon available, that does not mean that the recipe won't work. Also, beware of the cooking times indicated. Thermostats in domestic ovens vary from household to household. Use your eye, and especially your finger, to check for doneness. Professional cooks, with the exception of pastry cooks, almost never use specific times or timers.

The team that makes the chef. The Millcroft Inn, July 1987.

You want to acquire a 'feel' for your favourite foods.

Hot plates: Instructions frequently specify that plates or bowls should be warmed before serving. This apparently minor point, often neglected, can make all the difference between an adequate meal and a memorable one.

Herbs: Although all the recipes in this book call for fresh herbs, you may certainly substitute the dried variety. Dried herbs, however, are up to ten times stronger in flavour and must be used with caution.

A Word about Wines

Wines are a science in themselves. Although wine 'atlases', like encyclopedias, out-date themselves eventually, they are a sound and most gratifying investment. Unfortunately we do not have the same variety of wines available as in other countries, especially Europe. Special wines, if listed by the LCBO may be ordered through your local LCBO, or purchased from either 'vintage' or 'rare' wine stores.

• In my opinion it is both simple and pure, to drink, for instance, only champagne with a whole meal, providing the champagne is of good quality.

• There is also absolutely nothing wrong with drinking red wine with fish as long as the wine complements the dish. A fruity Alsatian wine is most appropriate with game and a slightly cool Beaujolais may very well be appropriate with salmon. Drink what you like and never mind what other people think.

• Try to serve Burgundy wines between 10° and 12°, white wines between 8° and 10°. Bordeaux wines should be served between 15° and 16°. Never place a wine near a source of heat to warm it up, you may create a process that will 'kill' the wine; instead, to bring an average wine to room temperature, put it in an 'unheated' room for 24 hours, the rest of the warming and 'breathing' process will happen in the glass.

• If you have an unusually rare wine and are not quite sure how to handle it, consult a professional who will be glad to advise you. In other words don't be proud, be practical. It may very well contribute to a once in a lifetime experience.

The Photographs

* Recipes for these desserts are too complex to include in a cookbook intended for home use. The reader is cordially invited to indulge a sweet tooth by visiting The Millcroft Inn in Alton where these items are occasionally included on the menu.

Glossary

to Blanch (v.)	Cook very quickly in hot liquid, then chill in ice water.
Blanquette (n.)	A highly seasoned stew prepared with a white-wine sauce.
Chartreuse (n.)	A mousseline mixture with a soft centre, baked in molds and elaborately garnished with vegetables. *Not* the pale green liqueur made by Carthusian monks.
Gnocchi (n.)	Potato dumplings. The semolina dough is rolled, cut in spheres and flattened with a fork. The dumplings are poached and/or baked.
Julienne (v.)	To cut in slivers or fine sticks. Often to do with vegetables.
Mousseline (n.)	A purée of ground fish, chicken or veal worked slowly over ice into a paste of eggs and cream. Delicate and short-lived.
Paupiette (n.)	A flattened slice of meat or fish rolled into an olive-shape; could also be a dollop of prepared mixture rolled in a vegetable leaf. Usually braised, roasted or sautéed.
Paysanne (v.)	To cut in large, squared-off slices.
Provençale (n.)	A crispy topping of breadcrumbs, melted butter and seasonings. For soups, omelettes, fish or meat. May also describe the use of Provence-herbs in a dish.
Quenelle (n.)	A small egg-shaped dumpling of mousseline, formed with two spoons and lightly poached in stock.
Sabayon (n.)	A frothy custard of egg yolks whipped with sugar, white wine and liqueur over a double boiler.
Sbrinz (n.)	A Swiss cheese similar to Parmesan, which may be used as a substitute.
Sweat (v.)	To toss in hot butter, quickly.

Index